LOUIS KOMZSIK

THREE OF LIFE

The perfect number

Trafford Publishing

THREE OF LIFE

The perfect number

Louis Komzsik

Order this book online at www.trafford.com
or email orders@trafford.com

Most Trafford titles are also available at major online book retailers.

Note for Librarians: A cataloguing record for this book is available from Library and Archives Canada at www.collectionscanada.ca/amicus/index-e.html

Printed in Victoria, BC, Canada.

ISBN: 978-1-4269-1859-9 (soft)
ISBN: 978-1-4269-1860-5 (hard)

Library of Congress Control Number: 2009936887

Our mission is to efficiently provide the world's finest, most comprehensive book publishing service, enabling every author to experience success. To find out how to publish your book, your way, and have it available worldwide, visit us online at www.trafford.com

Trafford rev. 10/15/2009

 www.trafford.com

North America & international
toll-free: 1 888 232 4444 (USA & Canada)
phone: 250 383 6864 ♦ fax: 812 355 4082

To those who wonder

Contents

Acknowledgments

Several people deserve my gratitude for reviewing the manuscript in its various stages. My long time colleagues, Wil Valenzuela and Paul Sicking gave me corrections that greatly contributed to the clarity of the book. Michelle Freret, a bright young high school senior, provided comments that validated and reinforced the intended level of presentation.

I am indebted to Olivier Schreiber, who does not seem to get tired of being a sounding board for my writing adventures and has an excellent eye for details. I also thank Ms. Latha Menon of Oxford University Press for her constructive critique of an early version of the manuscript.

Finally, I acknowledge the valuable contributions of Cathy Babcock, Stephen Weathers, Leya Taylor and Rian Anderson at Trafford Publishing.

The photographs in the book are from the Wikipedia Commons with their permission granted therein, except the photo of the tripteron at the temple of Zeus that I took on a recent trip to Athens.

August, 29, 2009
Louis Komzsik

Prologue

We live in a finite, small segment of an apparently infinite universe and we have long been fascinated by certain numbers that appear to have more relevant relationship to the universe than others. There is no simpler number that implies a deeper connection with the universe than the humble number three.

After all, the number three may be arrived at by simple counting, but it has a curious relationship with many universal phenomena appealing to the human sense of intrigue. This may explain the many everyday uses and human fascination with the number even though the actual reasons are shrouded in mystery.

This book discusses appearances of the number ranging from archaeological finds and religious symbols to biology and physics. Its main focus is, however, on the diverse mathematical roles of the number as a geometric and arithmetic building block as well as a gatekeeper of, or a gateway to infinity.

The intended reader of this book is the everyday person of all ages, from students to working adults, with some interest in history and mathematics. The mathematical discussion is kept as simple as possible, a high school mathematical background is sufficient to enjoy.

1

Of trilithons and tripterons

Perhaps the first archaeological demonstrations of the number three are the ancient trilithons (special arrangements of two vertical stone columns holding a horizontal stone slab), consisting of three stones. Archaeologists consider several sites of ancient architectural ruins as trilithons. Such are found in places in Malta in temple buildings, or in Egypt in the Valley of the Kings, also in temple constructions. In these cases they may only be doors or gates employing the structural convenience provided by the three member construction. There is another occurrence on the island of Maui in Hawaii, where it was a gateway into the royal gardens.

The most intriguing examples of trilithons are those of Stonehenge, one of them shown in Figure 1.1. They date back to about 4,500 years ago. There is mystery surrounding the construction of the trilithons. In most cases the stones used for construction were not found naturally in the vicinity of the trilithons and they had to be carried there from long distances. Their means of delivery is also fervently argued by archaeologists, but their actual construction is the biggest mystery.

Most of the stones are too big to handle manually or with tools operated by human power, no matter how ingenious they are. Stonehenge's trilithons range from 20 to 24 feet in height and their weight is around 50 tons. Digging holes for the two vertical stones is accepted to be the way, although raising them upright is still a superior feat of accomplishment. Putting the third stone on top of the two vertical ones is the real mystery, akin to the construction of the pyramids. Earthen ramp construction is reluctantly accepted as the solution, but only due to lack of any better explanation.

FIGURE 1.1 Trilithon of Stonehenge

If it is controversial how they were built, it is even more mysterious what purpose they served, a topic hotly contested by historians. The role of Stonehenge trilithons is clearly not that of a doorway. Their two vertical columns were placed very close to each other making it impossible to walk through between them. On the other hand they create a specific line of sight in a certain direction for a person standing in the middle of the arrangement. Stonehenge contains several trilithons arranged in directions to the sunrise and sunset at the winter and summer solstices, hence the most popular belief is that of Stonehenge having been a calendar type instrument based on some astronomical insight of the people of that time.

Besides the calendar role, many other hypotheses are held. One such is the role of Stonehenge being a destination of extra-terrestrials arriving from another star system. In this interpretation the circular shape of the arrangement of the five trilithons at Stonehenge somehow accommodated the alien spacecraft as a landing platform. The external stone circle comprised of single columns with no top stone would disperse the exhaust of the rocket propelling the space ship.

Yet again, some other people think that the arrangement was some kind of energy generator, or collector equipment. It is not a very big stretch of the imagination to see lenses placed in the openings of the gaps between the vertical columns and focusing their beams to the center point. As we all know from grade school physics exercises or brave backyard experiments, the focused light will generate enough heat at least to set paper afire.

Adding new hypotheses to the discussion on Stonehenge's role is not our goal here, we just needed to establish the fact that early humans went to extreme hardship to put three, not four, not two, but three

stones together in a peculiar arrangement. Whatever
the reasons were, still we wonder about the fact that
three stone columns were used.

Among the early archaeological hints at the fundamental building block nature of three is manifested in
the sanctuary of Zeus in Athens, built by Deucalion,
the first ruler of Greeks. The erection of the temple started in 515 BC, but soon the construction was
stopped. It was resumed only in 175 BC and was completed as an international effort with funding from the
king of Syria, Antioch the fourth, and by Roman architect Cassutius in Corinthian style (one of the three
dominant column styles of the times, the other two
being Doric and Ionic).

The temple was one of the largest of the ancient
world measuring 110 meters in length (well exceed-
ing the length of a football field) and 44 meters in
width. The ends of the temple were supported by
three rows of columns, called tripterons, whose rem-
nants are shown in Figure 1.2. The center contained a
very large golden and ivory statue of Zeus and that of
the emperor Hadrian, who at that time was worshiped
as an equal to Zeus.

Why three rows of columns were used may be explained by modern statical or architectural considerations, still one cannot but wonder if there was some
more divine reason in it. The temple suffered its first
serious damage in the 5th century AD and continued
to deteriorate during the centuries due to further natural disasters as well as human activities. The final
blow came in 1852 when an earthquake toppled one

FIGURE 1.2 The tripteron of the temple of Zeus in Athens

of the remaining 16 standing columns of the original 104 columns. That column is still visible lying on the ground today.

Organizing things into three parts, or building something from three components, is called trichotomy and it is both a philosophical and mathematical concept. The classical trichotomy of mathematics is the fact that there are only three possible relations between two numbers, a and b. They are $a < b$, $a = b$ and $a > b$. There are also commonly occurring triple inequalities of the form $x \leq y \leq z$, representing a trichotomy relation between three quantities. Mathematics, as we will see, is full of the occurrences of the number three.

The philosophical origins date back to the Greek philosopher Aristotle who lived in the 4th century BC. He was born in the Greek mainland, not to far from the

city of Thessaloniki. He extensively traveled through
the Greek territories and was invited to be the teacher
of Alexander the Great. Later he returned to Athens
and composed most of his great treatises that are still
available today. He studied and wrote about astronomy, physics, geography, philosophy, ethics, politics,
in other words he was a polyhistor.

One of his writings stated the three requisites of
beauty: wholeness, radiance and harmony. The words
have various shades of meaning resulting in different
interpretations, but there are three of them. Aristotle
also posited a trichotomy of the person in unity, truth
and goodness, another triple subject to interpretation.

Some ancient peoples considered the three fundamental substances being earth, water and fire. Earth
of course is the origin of life, the creator of some sort.
Water is sustaining all life on the Earth. Finally, fire
is the destroyer of things all living and earthen. This
was the foundation of religious trichotomies resulting
in various divine triads.

The Indian God Trimurti, for example, had three
heads manifesting the three phases of birth, life and
death with the three personalities of Brahma, Vishnu
and Shiva. An ancient carving of this, sometimes
called the Hindu trinity is shown in Figure 1.3. It
is easy to see the correspondence of earth and birth,
the water and life, as well as fire and death.

The most common belief is that Vishnu is in the center as the stage of life, while Shiva and Brahma represent birth and death on the sides. They fell apart into

FIGURE 1.3 The Trimurti

three beings during the ages and Brahma itself is not worshiped anymore, but both Vishnu and Shiva are actively followed. The trichotomy continues, Vishnu, the God of life, in turn has three incarnations in Krishna, Rama and Narayana.

Another triple deity was known to the Babylonians as Anu, Enlil and Enki, but the most notable triple manifestation of deity is the Trinity of Christianity, the Heavenly Father, the Son and the Holy Spirit. This belief system is aligned with the philosophical concept of the trichotomy of man stating that all of us are comprised of body, mind and spirit.

This trichotomy is vehemently contested by some scholars promoting a dichotomy instead, that of body and mind only. It is caused by the fact that the least understood and accepted component of the Christian

Trinity is the Holy Spirit. This probably stems from our trouble of distinguishing between our soul and our mind.

On the contrary, there are those who adhere to a tritheistic belief proposing that the Trinity is actually three distinct Gods. Incidentally most of the altar paintings of Christianity are triptychs, comprised of three partitions. Jesus, the second member of the Trinity is not anymore subject of academic polemy, it is widely accepted by even non-believers that Jesus was a living person. His life and teachings are described in detail in the New Testament and there is even archaeological support to some of the events attributed to his life.

Leading up to Jesus' birth is the story of the three, not four or two, wise men or kings, Melchior, Balthazar and Gaspar, who followed the star to Bethlehem. The tale of the wise men is not from the Bible, they are from references from the times AD. They were supposedly from the East, from Arabia and appeared bearing various gifts. Whether they were real or imaginary, it is important that there were three of them and left us with the wonderful custom of Christmas gifts.

There are numerous other notable occurrences of the number three in the Christian culture. Jesus had three temptations by Satan, had been denied thrice by Peter, there were three crucified on that fateful day and the resurrection occurred three days later. There were three nails used in the crucification and Jesus was of 33 years of age at the time. Then there are the Christian virtues of faith, hope and charity, three and three, again and again.

Following the thread, we can point out that God's major prophets numbered three: Moses, Jesus and Mohammed, leaving us the three main religions of our times, Judaism, Christianity and Islam. Despite the tremendous differences between the three, especially considering the current world atmosphere, they are in fact unified in the fact that they all worship a single entity of God.

The Muslim religion has three sacred cities in Mecca, Medina and Jerusalem, the latter being just as sacred to the other two main religions of the three, Christianity and Judaism. The fact that it is now located in a Jewish state contributes a lot to the political volatility of the Middle East. As the origins of all three, sometimes called Abrahamic, religions are geographically linked to this area for millennia, an expeditious solution is highly unlikely.

Let us finally look at the appearances of the number three in the ancient mythology and history. The Greek mythology had many references to the three Graces, presumably the daughters of Zeus, albeit there is some disagreement in that between various sources. These beautiful young women represented charm, beauty and creativity, like brains, beauty and personality in modern thinking. They were adored by artists and were subject of many medieval paintings and sculptures. Figure 1.4 is a section of Boticello's famous painting titled *Primavera* depicting the Graces.

We can find trichotomy in history. The Roman his-

FIGURE 1.4 The three Graces

tory already brought us the triumvirates of three rulers, the first organized by Julius Caesar in around 60 BC. Caesar's two partners were Marcus Crassus and Pompeius Magnus. In a cruel fate of life, two of the three (Pompeius and Caesar) were murdered and the third (Crassus) died on the battlefield, the concept, however remained alive.

There are so many historical references, it is impossible to gather them all in a book whose focus is not on the historical, but on the number's mathematical roles. The fact, however, that history is inundated with occurrences of the number three implies a deeper cause that is worthy of further examination.

2

One, two, three and counting

Let us now look at the road leading humans to the number three. It is unclear how counting first emerged in human thinking, but it appeared, very likely, in prehistoric times. In order to count, one needs to use some kind of repeating unit, and ancient peoples were able to observe such in the changing of days and the rising of Moon every night, and on a larger scale the seasons and the years. At the very beginning, say ten thousand years ago, it may have been the privilege of priests, shamans, medicine men and the likes to be able to grasp the concept of numbers. Soon, however, everybody must have learned to distinguish between the number of the people in his tribe versus others or the quantity of prey to hunt for food.

The road to the number three was also somewhat slow. At the very beginning of human counting in some ancient societies the first counts were: one, two and many. Even as recently as in the last century, the native African Hottentot tribe counted only to three, after three came more. For some thousands of years the number three was a gateway number for multiplicity! But after that, the floodgate was opened and humanity started to really count with what we call today the natural numbers, one, two, three, four and so on until infinity.

The ancient Chinese pioneered the art of arithmetic. They used counting boards for adding numbers and they even used two differently colored sticks, black and red, red signifying the number of sticks to be taken away from the black. Hence, the red sticks may be considered as the predecessors of negative numbers. The subtraction operation was executed by removing as many black sticks as red sticks were in the row below, with the appropriate carry-over in case of subtraction of a larger number from a smaller one.

The next logical desire was to "write" the numbers. The Chinese and Sumerians started record keeping of quantifiable goods, such as the emperor's concubines or the number of bushels of grains. The difficulties in establishing the exact history of numbers in that time period lies in the perishable nature of the writing materials. Papyrus and clay tables, used in these two cultures respectively, do not withstand extreme circumstances.

Writing numbers as we could call it today has certainly evolved from the simple marking of short lines, a clear indication of the time when counting was done with wooden sticks, to the system of Arabic numbers we use today. The Egyptians started from |, ||, |||, and so on and indicated more by certain positioning and repeating patterns. Their only other symbol was ∩ which stood for ten. The Babylonian cuneiform symbols were similar with the wider appearance of the stick on the top, indicating a bottom to top carving technique. In fact one of the hypotheses about the shape of the number three is that in cuneiform writing

the upper parts of the three lines may have touched
due to the shape of the tool and the image was rotated in later years.

The Mayans started with ., .., ... and used − for
five. The combinations for large numbers were easily obtained again by repeating and positioning. The
Chinese started from −, =, ≡ but then deviated into
different symbols, perhaps the first sign of symbolism
as opposed to counting. The Greeks used their al-
phabet letters for numbers and the Roman numbers
are well known as an extension of the Egyptian with
special symbols for five (V), ten (X), hundred (C), etc.

In many of these ancient notations the three was
the last distinct "counting" number sign and the reuse
of the symbols started after that. Most ancient and
modern notations use different symbols above three
and special positioning and repetitions thereafter, im-
plying the need for a rule above that level.

That rule, the place system, may have been invented
by the Chinese about four thousand years ago. It dates
back to the times, when counting was accomplished
by aforementioned wooden sticks placed on a board.
They used boxes on the counting board and different
amount of sticks placed in the boxes, up to the maximum of 5, which enabled definition of any number up
to 9 in a box. The first four were vertical, the five
was indicated by a horizontally placed stick, and so
on until 9, which was marked by ‖‖. The position
of the boxes indicated the place value. If the board
contained three boxes, the first had a place value of
a hundred, the second one ten and the rightmost one

of unity. The right justification on a board containing many boxes in a row defined a generalization that lead to the use of the boards with multiple rows of boxes as an efficient addition device.

The place system was also invented by the Sumerians and retained by their successors, the Babylonians. They adopted a system of base 60 (notably divisible by three). For example, written evidence suggests that their notation of a number, say, 1,2,3 had a numeric value of $1 + 2 \cdot 60 + 3 \cdot 60 \cdot 60$. In the notation here, for the sake of printability, "," denotes the separation of the digits.

There is archaeological evidence indicating that the place system with decimal numbers, or our decimal system, was also employed by the Hindu culture in India, around 4000 years ago, around the time of the Babylonians' takeover of the Sumerian empire and culture. Hence we do not know whose invention was the original, they may have been three co-inventors.

The fact that both positive and negative numbers were used and the place system was developed did not mean that the concept of zero had appeared. Far from it. There are clay tablets of ancient Babylonian origin with cuneiform writing that have numbers where certain powers of the base did not have a term. For example, the number we would write as 3601 today was written by the Babylonians as 1, , 1 or $1 \cdot 1 + 1 \cdot 60 \cdot 60$. The double comma indicates the missing term (the multiplier of 60), but there was no symbol for it.

It appears that sometimes in the first centuries AD

Hindu mathematicians introduced a symbol for the empty position in their place system. In some ancient Hindu manuscripts a dot indicated the empty position, an early predecessor to zero. Having a symbol for zero and considering it a number is, however, a rather big leap. The latter feat is also contributed to the Indians but much much later.

The Indian Brahmagupta lived in the northwest region of India during the 7th century AD. He was a professional astronomer and he ran an observatory, but he was very active in mathematics and wrote several texts that were widely known at the time. He was mainly interested in geometry and there is a formula named after him regarding the area of quadrilateral shapes inscribed in a circle. Working with circles he needed to use π occasionally and incidentally he used 3 as the approximate value for π. More on this topic a little bit later.

He appears to have been the first to lay down some arithmetic rules involving zero. He recognized and stated that adding positive and negative numbers of the same magnitude results in zero, or that adding zero to anything did not change a thing. He ran into trouble when trying to divide by zero, as many since then (even nowadays), but nevertheless, he was the first to do correct arithmetic operations involving zero.

The Indian work eventually became known in the Arabic countries and was described in a text by the Persian Al' Khwarizmi in the 9th century AD. His life history is not really known except for the fact that his name, known in several close variations in different

sources, implies his birthplace to have been somewhere
in a region of the Persian empire that is part of Uze-
bekhistan these days. He apparently spent his professional years in the library of Baghdad, then a central
place for scholarly research.

His works summarized his knowledge of solutions to
linear and quadratic equations. They were translated
to Latin sometimes in the 12th century and became
the origin of the "Arabic" numbers we use today. The
Latin version of his name (Algorismus) is considered to
be the origin of the word algorithm. The book spread
into Europe (very slowly) but ultimately reached the
whole continent. Some parts of it, like the zero itself,
still had not been widely accepted, and it took a few
hundred years before it truly penetrated the mathematical thinking everywhere.

Another, very important concept is the fraction. Almost as soon as counting permeated the thinking of
humankind, the need for the ability to describe a part
of the whole must have also appeared. The need to
divide some food between the members of a family resulted in unit fractions, i.e., one half, one third, one
fourth of a whole and so on. Since these fractions all
have one in the numerator, an easy notation arose in
Egypt. The Egyptians used a dot on the top of a num-
ber to indicate the unit fraction, for example, $\dot{|||}$ would
indicate one third or $\frac{1}{3}$ in modern notation.

The Egyptians carried this into science by expressing
non-unit fractions as sums of unit fractions. This also
required a certain arithmetic skill, specifically addition
and subtraction. They developed specific rules to do

so, rules that would not pass today's scrutiny as they sometimes fail. Nevertheless, the Egyptians correctly computed $\frac{2}{7} = \frac{1}{4} + \frac{1}{28}$ and similar non-unit fractions. Their rules included summing up to four unit fractions to produce a non-unit fraction.

In the context of fractions our number 3 suddenly appears as a gateway to infinity. When dividing 1 by 3 we obtain the first fractional number that has an infinite number of digits:

$$\frac{1}{3} = 0.333333... = 0.\dot{3}.$$

The notation of the dot over the three on the right hand side indicates an infinite repetition of the digit.

Furthermore, division of natural numbers by 3 produces an infinite sequence of single digits of either 0, 3, or 6 as

$$1/3 = 0.\dot{3}, \ 2/3 = 0.\dot{6}, \ 3/3 = 1.\dot{0},$$

$$4/3 = 1.\dot{3}, \ 5/3 = 1.\dot{6}, \ 6/3 = 2.\dot{0},$$

and so on. The concept of the fraction led to a class of non-natural numbers called rational numbers. These numbers can always be written as the ratio of two integer numbers. The integer numbers are comprised of the natural numbers and their negative counterparts.

The number 3 has other interesting divisional properties. A natural number is divisible by 3 if the sum of its digits is divisible by 3. The simple example of 12 demonstrates this fact; the sum of its digits is 3, which is obviously divisible by 3. Another example is the number 18, with sum of digits (9) that is divisible by 3. Incidentally, it follows that the numbers obtained from a number divisible by 3 via the reversal of the order of digits are also divisible by 3. Just consider 21 and 81 in connection with the above examples.

It is very easy to prove by simple mathematical means this divisibility rule. Let us consider an integer number n written as

$$n = d_0 + d_1 \cdot 10 + d_2 \cdot 100 + d_3 \cdot 1000 \ldots$$

where the d_i are the digits of the number. Then the sum of the digits is

$$sum = d_0 + d_1 + d_2 + d_3 + \ldots$$

Subtracting these two results in

$$n - sum = 9 \cdot d_1 + 99 \cdot d_2 + 999 \cdot d_3 + \ldots$$

On the right hand side all the numbers are divisible by 3 because $9, 99, 999, \ldots$ are all divisible by 3. Then from

$$n = sum + 9 \cdot d_1 + 99 \cdot d_2 + 999 \cdot d_3 + \ldots$$

it follows that n is divisible by 3 if the sum of the digits is also divisible by 3. For example, 12345 should be divisible because the sum of its digits, 15, is divisible. Surely $12345/3 = 4115$. The special nature of the otherwise common fractions generated by 3 and the divisibility of whole numbers by 3 are rather curious, but less noteworthy in light of things to come.

We are surprised by the sudden appearance of the infinity in connection with the number three, but it is

possible that we are not looking at it in the right frame
of reference, i.e., the universe's, whatever that may be.
Its mysterious properties may not be in the number itself, but in our interpretation of it. That would explain
our lack of full comprehension of the role of the number
three and its gateway nature to infinity. It is possible
that our decimal number system, evolved based on our
bodies and the resulting ten digits on our hands, may
not be the right system to see some numbers and their
intrinsic role meaningfully. For example, the representation of the number 0.333... with infinite number of
repeated digits would be simply 0.1 in a base 3 system.

Let's see, how such system would work. A base three
system would only have three digits: $0, 1, 2$ and their
value would agree with their decimal system counterparts. The number 3, however, would be 10 in a base
three system, interpreted as $1 \cdot 3 + 0 \cdot 1$. Following
this logic $0.3333... = 1/3$ in decimal would be 0.1 in
the base three system, presented as $0 \cdot 1 + 1 \cdot 3^{-1}$ or
$0 \cdot 1 + 1 \cdot \frac{1}{3}$. Despite the advantages of some number
presented with infinite number of decimal digits being
represented with finite digits in a base three system,
such a system is somewhat counterintuitive for us, ten-
digited humans.

There are many other trichotomies in various mathematical branches. For example, there are three means
or averages in statistics. They are the well known
arithmetic mean of two numbers as $f = (a + b)/2$,
the appealing geometric mean of $g = \sqrt{ab}$, and the
seldom used harmonic mean of $h = 2ab/(a + b)$. These
three definitions may also be extended to any number
of terms.

Finally, we view the number three's peculiar proximity to a very special number, the number π and three being the basis for many approximations to it. One of the most intriguing approximations of π is the continuous fraction involving three in the form of

$$\pi = 3 + \cfrac{1^2}{3 \cdot 2 + \cfrac{3^2}{3 \cdot 2 + \cfrac{5^2}{3 \cdot 2 + \cfrac{7^2}{3 \cdot 2 + \ldots}}}}.$$

The repetitive anchoring appearance role of three implies an intrinsic relationship between a member of the simplest kind of numbers, the natural numbers, and the beguiling number π. And this is only the forerunner of many intriguing coincidences to come.

The number three will also have an important role in the solution of the three famous unsolved problems of antiquity, the squaring the circle, the trisecting of angles and the doubling of a cube, the subjects of the next chapter.

3

Three challenges of antiquity

Three challenging problems captured the fantasy of many people throughout the ages and had tremendous influence on the development of geometry. The solution of these problems obsessed generations of geometers through millennia. Many believed that they obtained a solution to the problem only to be proven faulty later.

The first and most widely known problem of squaring the circle sought a square whose area is the same as that of a given circle by means of a construction using only a straight edge ruler and a compass. This problem was already described in a document nowadays known as the Rhind papyrus. The document was copied by an Egyptian scribe named Ahmes from an ancient papyrus manuscript from around the 17th century BC.

We do not know too much about Ahmes himself, but he appears to have been well versed in arithmetics. He described many of the methods Egyptians used to generate unit fractions, a subject briefly mentioned in the last chapter. In the Rhind document Ahmes gave the following solution to the problem: 8/9th of the circle's diameter is the side of the square. This gave a reasonable approximation for π as $256/3^4 = 3.16$, which is accurate for one decimal digit, compared to 3.14. Notice the number three peeking through the formula.

The desired solution of the problem would be, however, to construct the segment of the length of $\sqrt{\pi}$, if for example we consider a unit circle, with the classical means of a straight ruler and a compass. Figure 3.1 depicts the challenge. The π is one of the most beguiling numbers humankind ever encountered. It is obviously not an integer, but if it was a rational number, one could possibly accomplish the feat of constructing it.

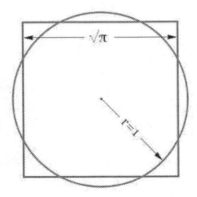

FIGURE 3.1 The problem of squaring the circle

After centuries of fruitless work, it was grudgingly understood that π is not a rational number. The Swiss mathematician Lambert in 1761 proved that π is irrational. Irrational numbers, as their name clearly indicates, simply cannot be written as the ratio of two integers numbers. But that was not the end of the story.

Transcendental numbers were classified by the French Liouville in the 1840s as such numbers that cannot be the solutions of algebraic equations with integer coefficients. This is a restriction much more severe than even the class of irrational numbers. The transcendental nature of π would certainly make the problem of squaring the circle, impossible to solve with the classical geometric means of a straight edge ruler and a compass.

The transcendental nature of π was finally proven by the German mathematician Lindemann in 1881. The squaring problem that occupied the minds of mathematicians for many centuries was put to rest. Or was it?

There are, of course other ways to solve the problem if we release the construction conditions of straight edge and compass as shown in Figure 3.2. The unit circle of the left hand side is rolled on the horizontal line half of a full rotation, or 180 degrees. The marked quarter of the circle enables us to follow that motion. Then the distance between points A and B is half of the circumference of the circle, or π.

From the terminal location of the rotated circle it follows that the BC distance is unity. Let us draw a half circle with diameter of $\overline{AC}$. A vertical line from point B intersects the half circle at point D. Since the ABD and DBC triangles are similar, the ratio of their corresponding sides are the same:

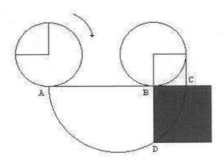

FIGURE 3.2 Squaring the circle

$$\frac{\overline{AB}}{\overline{BD}} = \frac{\overline{BD}}{\overline{BC}}$$

from which it follows that

$$\overline{AB} \cdot \overline{BC} = \overline{BD}^2.$$

Since $\overline{BC} = 1$ by the virtue of the unit circle and $\overline{AB} = \pi$ from the construction, it follows that

$$\overline{BD} = \sqrt{\pi}.$$

We found the square of side $\overline{BD}$ whose area is equal to the unit circle. The process of obtaining it was not entirely a geometric construction since the rolling of the circle is a logical (and possibly manual) process, but we solved the problem exactly.

The second of the three ancient challenges was the trisection of angles with straight ruler and compass. Trisection is the division of an angle into three equal angles. Trisection of certain angles is obviously possible by those classical means. The trisection of a hundred eighty degree angle into three sixty degree angles by measuring up the radius on the circumference of a circle with a compass is well known.

The trisection of an arbitrary angle, however, is impossible by those means. Easing up on the restriction a bit by allowing a marking on the ruler enables the solution of the problem, as was found by Hippocrates in the fifth century BC. He was born in Chios, Greece and he was a geometer whose work produced several gems, like the solution to the trisection problem. He is sometimes confused with his contemporary of the same name, who lived most of his life on the island of Kos in Greece. The other Hippocrates was a physician, known as the father of medicine.

Hippocrates constructed a trisection as shown in Figure 3.3. Given the angle CAB at a vertex A of a line segment AB, measure the $\overline{AC}$ distance onto the ruler, twice, resulting in three markings with the distance $\overline{AC}$ between each pair. Drawing a line through point C parallel to the line AB results in line FC. Finally, anchoring the first point of the marked ruler at A and rotating it from the vertical until the third mark is right on the FC line marks the location of the point E. The angle EAB is one third of the original angle CAB.

The fact may be proven by simple geometrical logic

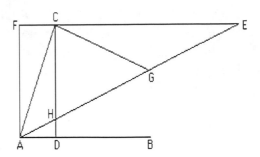

FIGURE 3.3 Trisecting angles

of exploring the equilateral triangles created in the construction process, such as CGE. Its details are omitted, since the important fact is the result that by allowing marking on the ruler, any angle my be trisected by construction. An ancient geometric problem solved with a minor improvement of the tool used or a relaxation of the rigid construction requirements.

The third ancient challenge was the doubling of a cube with the aid of only a straight edge ruler and a compass. The problem was to find the side of a cube that is of twice the volume of a given cube. Algebraically this is very simply stated as

$$b^3 = 2a^3,$$

where b is the yet unknown side of the double cube and a is the side of the given cube. It is easy to see that the solution is

$$b = \sqrt[3]{2}a.$$

Here the $\sqrt[3]{2}$ is the cubic root of 2. Just as squaring the square root of a number yields the original number, the cubic root of a number raised to the third power would produce the original number. Simply

$$(\sqrt[3]{2})^3 = 2.$$

Now if the number $\sqrt[3]{2}$ can be constructed, then the double cube can also be constructed. Again, the problem cannot be solved with the unmarked straight edge and the compass.

The doubling of the cube problem was first also attacked by Hippocrates, who as we recall solved the trisection problem with a bit of trick. His geometric statement of an equivalent problem was as follows: For two given parallel lines l_1 and l_2, find two intermediate parallel lines x and y between them such that they are related as

$$l_1 : x = x : y = y : l_2.$$

Hippocrates proposed that if these two lines may be constructed, then the doubling of the cube may be accomplished. We do not know of his success in constructing the two lines. It was not very clear at his time why his statement was true.

Menaechmus in the fourth century BC followed Hippocrates' idea and presented it in algebraic terms. He was another representative of the extremely rich collection of ancient Greek geometers, born in a city that resides in modern day Turkey. His work focused on the conic sections: ellipse, parabola and hyperbola; in fact he is credited with their discovery. He used conic sections to solve many geometry problems, including the problem of doubling the cube.

Following Menaechmus' work and assuming for simplicity that $l_1 = 1$ and $l_2 = 2$ we can write

$$\frac{1}{x} = \frac{x}{y} = \frac{y}{2}.$$

This may be boiled down to two pairs of equations

$$\frac{1}{x} = \frac{y}{2} \rightarrow xy = 2$$

and

$$\frac{x}{y} = \frac{y}{2} \rightarrow y^2 = 2x.$$

They represent a hyperbola and a parabola, respectively. Their intersection gives

$$y^2 = 2\frac{2}{y} \rightarrow y^3 = 4.$$

The solution for the first line is

$$x = \frac{2}{y} = \sqrt[3]{2},$$

the crucial number required for the doubling. While the analogy now makes the geometric proposition well justified, it appears that we just traded construction with lines for intersecting conic sections, an even more difficult problem.

Insofar we honored, and will continue to honor, the ancient geometers with brief details of their biography to put their lives and accomplishments into a chronological and cultural context. If one of the modern scientists in the second millennium also deserves the same treatment, it is Isaac Newton. He was born in 1643 in Lincolnshire, England and died in 1727. His work titled *Philosophiae Naturalis Principia Mathematica* published in 1687 is probably the most influential scientific book ever written. He had spectacular contributions to physics, especially mechanics and he invented the calculus branch of mathematics. Both of these topics will have further mention in future pages.

Newton also left behind a treasure chest of mathematical gems, like the ingenious solution he proposed for doubling the cube shown in Figure 3.4. He used a simple relief from the original rules to allow a unit length marking on the ruler.

The construction starts from an equilateral triangle with unit length sides, or an equilateral triangle may be drawn, whose side will produce the unit length marking of the ruler. Let the vertices of this triangle be A, B and C. Extending the side AB and measuring the unit on it from vertex B results in point D. Drawing a line through D and C and extending it indefinitely in the direction of the arrow produces one of the construction lines. Also extending the BC side indefinitely in the direction of the arrow produces another one. Finally, anchoring the ruler at point A, rotating and sliding until its unit distance section is exactly between the two extended construction lines (i.e. $\overline{GH} = 1$) produces the segment $\overline{AG}$. That is of the length desired, $\overline{AG} = \sqrt[3]{2}$.

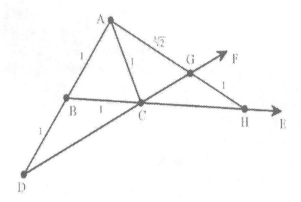

FIGURE 3.4 Doubling the cube

This may be proven by a geometric logic involving equilateral triangles and applying trigonometry based on their angles. Its details are beyond our focus here, but Newton's genius and internal vision is clear in the solution.

In conclusion, it appears that all three unsolved problems of antiquity were solved in certain ways, but none of them was solved by the originally required means of the time of the posing of them. The implicit role of three in the solution of these problems was via its geometric manifestation in triangles, the subject of the next chapter.

4

Triangles of the Greek geometers

The ancient Greek geometers held triangles in very high regard, and they exploited the fact that three points not located on the same line define a plane. Such three points could also specify a unique circle going through them. It was well known to the geometers that the triangle was the only perfect shape that when built into a mechanical device never changed its shape even if the corner-points had hinges, unless of course the sides were bent. This lent significance to triangles in ancient building construction practices.

Pythagoras, the doyen of the Greek geometers, was born on the island of Samos in Greece, but lived most of his life in Croton, that is part of modern day Italy, during the 6th century BC. He ran a school to study mathematics and live according to very strict principles. His school was open to women as well, a fact highly unusual at the time when women were still considered property. His tremendous influence survived the ages despite the fact that no written copy of his work has ever been found.

He is most famous for his theorem stating that the sum of the squares of the sides of a right triangle equals the square of the hypotenuse. The theorem was apparently known to the Babylonians much earlier, but

Pythagoras is credited with its proof for all right triangles. The triangle with sides 3, 4, and 5 demonstrates the theorem since $3^2 + 4^2 = 5^2$. This is the only set of three consecutive integers demonstrating the theorem and it is sometimes called the Pythagorean triple.

Pythagoras actually called the number three "the perfect number" not only because it anchored his triple, but because he recognized the specific role the number plays in many mathematical concepts, theorems, hypotheses and conjectures. His designation of the number three is clearly worthy of being the subtitle of this book.

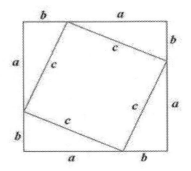

FIGURE 4.1 Pythagorean theorem

The theorem is very easy to prove by simple means as shown in Figure 4.1 equating the area of a square with the area of its interior partitions. The partitions consist of a smaller square and four identical triangles with a total area of

$$c^2 + 4\frac{ab}{2}.$$

The area of the big square with sides of $a + b$ is

$$(a + b)^2 - a^2 + b^2 + 4\frac{ab}{2}.$$

Since they occupy the same geometrical region, they are identical which implies the truth of the theorem

$$c^2 = a^2 + b^2.$$

Some records indicate that the Egyptians used ropes with knots marked at 3, 4 and 5 units apart, hence of 12 units length, to use during the construction of the pyramids to measure out right triangles, also called Egyptian triangles. It is apparent that the geometric manifestation of the three in the shape of a triangle permeated the thinking of humankind from a very early age.

Pythagoras sought relations between the triangle and certain numbers. He classified some numbers as triangular numbers, the first few being

$$3, 6, 10, 15, ...$$

This classification was based on the geometric pattern of the numbers, such as

1

1 1

$$1\ 1\ 1$$

$$1\ 1\ 1\ 1$$

which obviously produces 10 as $1 + 2 + 3 + 4$. He also recognized the special relationship between the sums of the odd numbers and the square numbers, $1 + 3$ summing to 4, $1 + 3 + 5$ producing 9 and so on like

$$1 + 3 + 5 + 7 = 16.$$

Another noteworthy triangular pattern of numbers is the triangle now known as Pascal's triangle that was also known to the Chinese in ancient times. The triangle is now attributed to the French mathematician of the 17th century, who according to anecdotal evidence came upon the numbers while trying to solve a gambling problem. The numbers are computed as the sum of the two terms above and the triangle is bound by one-s on the side:

$$1$$

$$1\ 1$$

$$1\ 2\ 1$$

$$1\ 3\ 3\ 1$$

$$\cdots$$

They correspond to the coefficients of the binomial expressions

$$(a + b)^0 = 1$$
$$(a + b)^1 = 1 \cdot a + 1 \cdot b$$
$$(a + b)^2 = 1 \cdot a^2 + 2 \cdot ab + 1 \cdot b^2$$
$$(a + b)^3 = 1 \cdot a^3 + 3 \cdot a^2 b + 3 \cdot ab^2 + 1 \cdot b^3$$

. . .

It is remarkable that the Pascal triangle's third terms from the left and the right starting from the fifth row contain all the Pythagorean triangular numbers, shown by the bold numbers as follows:

1 4 **6** 4 1

1 5 **10 10** 5 1

1 6 **15** 20 **15** 6 1

1 7 **21** 35 35 **21** 7 1

. . .

Triangles themselves exhibit several trichotomies. Classification by the angles results in obtuse, right and acute triangles. Another classification is based on the measure of the sides. The isoceles and equilateral triangles exhibit two and three identical length sides, respectively. The general triangle, called scalene triangle is one with three sides of different lengths. The special shape triangles captured large interest and were studied in detail throughout the millennia.

The most important may be the equilateral triangle (a triangle with equal sides) as it is the building block of three dimensional objects, the regular solids, discussed in a later chapter. The equilateral triangle is also a geometric source for another special number, subject of reverence through the ages, the golden ratio. This ratio is simply defined as the subdivision of unity where the ratio of the two parts is the same as the ratio of the larger part to unity. Algebraically it is defined as

$$\frac{1}{x} = \frac{x}{1-x}.$$

A simple reordering results in the quadratic equation

$$x^2 + x - 1 = 0,$$

whose solution obtained by the well known formula is

$$x = \frac{\sqrt{5} - 1}{2}.$$

This is the golden ratio, sometimes called the divine proportion. It was (and still is) assumed to be extremely attractive to humans esthetically. Many artists used it, for example Leonardo in his famous sketch of the human figure with the arms stretched.

Some also believe that certain dimensional ratios in the pyramids also adhere to the golden ratio, but that is somewhat speculative as those ratios were calculated from distances measured in some obscure units. To obtain the value geometrically appears to be difficult as $\sqrt{5}$ is an irrational number expressible only by infinite number of digits, clearly a huge inconvenience. In order to use the number in art, however, one needs a way to obtain it by geometric means, with a compass and a straight ruler. That turned out to be rather easy with the help of, surprise, the equilateral triangle.

Drawing a circle with a compass around a point O and starting from an arbitrary point on the circle (A), we use the radius to repeatedly mark five consecutive points (B, C, D, E, F). Connecting points A, C and E,

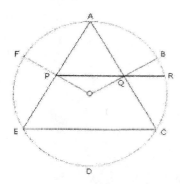

FIGURE 4.2 Golden ratio in triangle

we obtain an equilateral triangle shown in Figure 4.2.

Connecting points B and O, then F and O, the intersections with the sides of the triangle produce points P and Q, respectively. Finally, connecting these two points and extending to the circle, one obtains the point R. These three points define the golden ratio in geometric terms

$$\frac{\overline{PQ}}{\overline{PR}} = \frac{\overline{QR}}{\overline{PQ}},$$

where the line over the letters indicate the length of the segment between the points indicated by the letters.

Triangles produced one of the most astonishing improvements in medieval art, the appearance of the third dimension (in itself the topic of a later chap-

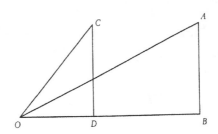

FIGURE 4.3 Euclid's optical triangles

ter) in paintings. In this case the triangle was truly a gateway to infinity via the projection triangle.

Euclid, one of the best known names in geometry, was another Greek geometer, now universally accepted as the father of geometry. He lived around 300 BC in Alexandria, at the time a Greek territory. We do not know much about the details of his life, however, many of his works survived. His main work, *Elements*, in essence lays the foundation for our geometry.

Another work of Euclid's, titled *Optics*, established an optical zero at the location of the eye (O) and the relative sizes of two objects ($\overline{AB}, \overline{CD}$) were measured by drawing two right triangles with a common baseline $\overline{OB}$, see Figure 4.3. The larger the angle at the eye-point was, the closer the object was physically or if the objects were at the same distance, the larger the object was.

Piero Della Francesca, an Italian artist of note in the 15th century carried the projection triangles even further. He recognized that given a unique point above a straight line segment divided into several parts, another line parallel to the first may be divided into the same proportions by connecting the unique point with the dividing points as shown in Figure 4.4.

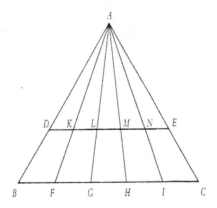

FIGURE 4.4 Piero's projection triangles

The unique point (A) became the "optical infinity", also known as the vanishing point. It is like when standing on a very straight road and looking into the distance the road appears to be narrower and narrower until it collapses into a point. We know that this is only a visual effect, and the road is of the same width

all the way. Carrying this concept back into art is
credited to Piero.

Piero's process started by establishing the infinite
point A and the width of his closest image $\overline{BC}$. He
also established the location of an image in the distance with the line $\overline{DE}$. Any subdivision in the fore-
front (F, G, H, I) was then projected towards infinity
via triangles as shown in Figure 4.4 producing a vi-
sually correct proportional subdivision in the distance
as K, L, M, N. His paintings utilizing this method became huge successes and he was rapidly followed by
other artists.

The triangle despite its simplicity had a huge impact
as a geometric object and will also be the foundation
of a bridge from geometry to algebra by way of the
trigonometry, subject of the next chapter.

5

The trigonometric bridge

Soon after satisfying their interest in the elementary geometry properties of triangles and exploiting most of the interesting properties of the Pythagorean theorem, the ancient geometers turned their attention to the angles of the right triangles. The concept of measuring the relationship between the sides and the angles of triangles led to the branch of mathematics we call trigonometry today. The name comes from Greek and loosely translates into measuring three angles.

In a right triangle, the sides adjacent to the right (90 degree) angle are denoted with a, b and the side opposite the right angle, called the hypotenuse is denoted with c in Figure 5.1. The angle opposite side a is α and the angle opposite side b is called β.

Several simple measures were defined very early. The ratio of one side adjacent to the right angle versus the hypotenuse was called the sine and defined as

$$sin(\alpha) = \frac{a}{c}.$$

The ratio of the other side adjacent to the right angle versus the hypotenuse became the cosine, i.e.

$$cos(\alpha) = \frac{b}{c}.$$

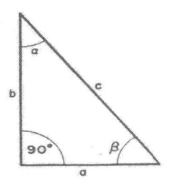

FIGURE 5.1 Right triangle

The direct ratio of the two adjacent sides was named tangent, and based on the two prior definitions was easily computed by simply dividing them. This basis was adequate to produce a framework that is widely used today in all aspects of life ranging from simple everyday applications to the most extreme scientific computations. It is hard not to marvel at the generality provided by this simplest of geometric objects and the influence of this foundation. It is, after all, used in computations that have nothing to do with triangles. Before we embark on the investigation of such, we'll widen the framework.

It is very easy to see that the *sin* function of one of the angles in the right triangle is the *cos* function of the other angle and vice versa. Since the sum of the angles in the triangle is 180 degrees, in the right triangle where the largest angle is 90 degrees, the sum of the other two angles is also 90 degrees. They are called each other's complementary angles and following relations hold between them:

$$sin(\beta) = sin(90 - \alpha) = cos(\alpha),$$

$$cos(\beta) = cos(90 - \alpha) = sin(\alpha).$$

Until now only functions of angles up to 90 degrees were defined. This may be generalized to angles beyond 90 degrees with specific sign conventions as shown in Figure 5.2 where s denotes $sin(\alpha)$, c the $cos(\alpha)$ and the circle is of unit radius.

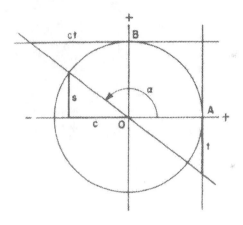

FIGURE 5.2 Generalization of trigonometric functions

This extension results in very important trigonometric identities used in a variety of applications. An angle and its difference from 180 degrees are called supple-

mentary angles. It is easy to see that the sine of an
angle α in the second quadrant of the coordinate system is the same as in the first, resulting in the relation

$$sin(180 - \alpha) = sin(\alpha).$$

The cosine of the complementary angle, since it is
aligned with the negative x axis, differs only in a sign

$$cos(180 - \alpha) = -cos(\alpha).$$

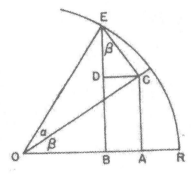

FIGURE 5.3 Trigonometric functions of two angles

Finally one can even extend the basic trigonometric functions to multiple angles. Using Figure 5.3 it
is easy to find the trigonometric functions of the sum
or difference of two angles. Assuming that the radius
in the figure is unity, we measure the two angles from
the horizontal axis consecutively, resulting in the point

E. Drawing a vertical line from E, we obtain point B. Measuring the angle β from this vertical line and intersecting with the original line of the β angle, we obtain C. Drawing a horizontal from C intersects the EB line at point D.

Using the previously defined elementary trigonometric functions in triangles OAC and EDC, respectively, it follows that

$$sin(\alpha+\beta) = BE = DE+AC = EC\cos(\beta)+OC\sin(\beta)$$
$$= sin(\alpha)cos(\beta) + cos(\alpha)sin(\beta).$$

By similar considerations we can derive the sum formula for the cosine as

$$cos(\alpha+\beta) = OB = OA-CD = OC\cos(\beta)-EC\sin(\beta)$$
$$= cos(\alpha)cos(\beta) - sin(\alpha)sin(\beta).$$

Given a certain angle, the trigonometric functions of the double of the angle may easily be obtained by substituting α for β in the above formulae as

$$sin(2\alpha) = sin(\alpha)cos(\alpha) + cos(\alpha)sin(\alpha)$$
$$= 2sin(\alpha)cos(\alpha),$$

and

$$cos(2\alpha) = cos(\alpha)cos(\alpha) - sin(\alpha)sin(\alpha)$$
$$= cos^2(\alpha) - sin^2(\alpha).$$

We now return to the idea of applications not necessarily related to triangles. Replacing α by 2α in the double angle formulae above enables the creation of triple angle formulae, or continuing the process for any

n-tuples. These lead to a most valuable approximation
concept, the trigonometric approximation of periodic
functions originated by French mathematician Fourier
in the early 19th century. He was as much a politi-
cian as mathematician, in fact he was a nobleman, a
Baron. At one point of his life Napoleon named him
the Governor of Lower Egypt. But his name is forever known by mathematicians and engineers for his
approximation and transformation techniques.

The Fourier series approximates a periodic function
$y = f(x)$ with the sum of an infinite number of sine
and cosine functions of increasingly higher orders:

$$y = a_0 + a_1 cos(\alpha) + b_1 sin(\alpha) + a_2 cos(2\alpha) + b_2 sin(2\alpha) + \ldots$$

The expression of a function in this form is called a
harmonic series. In practice, the series is stopped after
a certain number of terms. The key in this approximation strategy is that the function must exhibit a periodic behavior, i.e. a regularly repeated pattern. Such
a function of repeating pattern is specified by three
(again) quantities, a constant amplitude of the peaks
of the function, a period of repeated behavior, and a
starting phase. The period may also be described in
the form of a frequency of repetitions in a certain time
interval.

Many physical phenomena exhibit such behavior, and
while they cannot be described with a mathematical
closed form function they may be adequately expressed
in terms of a Fourier series. This renders trigonometry
to be one of the most important foundations of engineering computations.

Trigonometry was insofar described in terms of planar triangles. The principle can also be extended onto any non-planar surface, for example to the surface of a sphere. This is called spherical trigonometry, and since we live on a by and large spherical Earth, its usefulness is immense.

Great circles on a sphere are such whose plane cuts through the center of the sphere. For example, on Earth the longitudinal (North-South) lines are great circles. The latitudes in general are not, except for the equator. Three intersecting great circles on the sphere define a spherical triangle. Such could be attained by two longitudinal lines and the equator as shown in Figure 5.4.

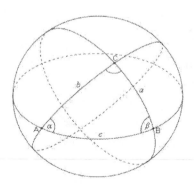

FIGURE 5.4 Spherical triangle

It is intuitively clear that the sum of the three angles of this spherical triangle is more than 180 degrees.
The amount above 180 degrees is a quantity called the
spherical access. This could be a nontrivial amount,
for example consider the case where the AC side is the
90 degree longitude while the BC side is the zero degree (at Greenwich) and corners A and B are on the
equator while C is the North Pole. All three angles are
90 degrees and their sum is 270 resulting in a spherical
access of 90 degrees.

The concept of a spherical right triangle is also valid.
Having one side on the equator and one side a longitudinal line guarantees one right angle at their intersection. Specifying a third side on a great circle that
is not longitudinal, and there is an infinite number of
them, creates a spherical right triangle.

Ultimately all the planar trigonometric relations may
also be defined on a spherical triangle and a world of
computational opportunities had been spawned from
this generalization. The contribution of trigonometry to describe our immediate surroundings, the Earth
with its lone natural and many man-made satellites, is
priceless.

Practical trigonometry has permeated history ever
since the early days. A famous practical trigonometrist
was Archimedes, who lived between 287-212 BC. He
was born, spent his life and died in Syracuse in Sicily,
at the time also a Greek territory. The firm dates of
his life are known because he became widely known
already in his life. His heroic feats in defending his
home town against the invading Romans were extolled

at length in many texts. One of his accomplishments was building machines that catapulted stones for very large distances, no doubt the beginning of ballistic science. In fact he died defending his town, killed by a Roman soldier while working on some mathematical problem drawn in the sand of his backyard. His last words according to some historical records were: "Do not bother my circles".

He is considered to be one of the greatest mathematicians of all times, certainly way ahead of his contemporaries. He was the first to utilize trigonometry to solve practical problems and could be considered the first applied mathematician ever. For example, in order to establish the proper angle of the catapult setting to reach a ship at a particular distance, he used trigonometric calculations. He is credited with using fraction approximations for the radical numbers necessary for some angles. For example, for the value of

$$sin(60) = \frac{\sqrt{3}}{2},$$

he used the approximation of

$$\frac{265}{153} < \sqrt{3} < \frac{1351}{780}.$$

This is still an amazingly good approximation for the square root of the number three, and is useful for everyday use. Even more important is the insight of bounding the number from above and below, enabling a practical error evaluation, a concept far ahead of its time when he lived.

Finally, let us revisit Figure 5.3 and view the right triangle OBE. Applying the Pythagorean theorem produces

$$\overline{OB}^2 + \overline{BE}^2 = \overline{OE}^2.$$

Since the hypotenuse OE is of unit length, by applying the sine and cosine functions appropriately for the angle $x = \alpha + \beta$ gives the famous Pythagorean identity of trigonometry

$$sin^2(x) + cos^2(x) = 1.$$

This identity opens up a wealth of possibilities in expressing trigonometric functions with each other, to solve algebraic equations and integrals by trigonometric substitutions. These topics are outside of our focus, but they are attesting to the power emanating from the simple number three and its geometric manifestation, the triangle.

6

Triangulation and triangularization

A useful application of triangles is in processes called triangulation. One of the triangulation processes aims to find unmeasurable distances of far objects by measuring certain angles and using trigonometry.

One of the first known attempts at using triangles to measure unmeasurable objects was done by the Greek Thales in the 6th century BC. He lived in the town of Miletos which is now a Turkish territory but was Greek land at the time of his life. Thales was mainly known as a philosopher with some interest in geometry as well as in astronomy. There are some written records indicating that he actually predicted a solar eclipse that occurred during his lifetime.

Thales is most known after his theorem related to triangles drawn on the diameter of a circle as one side. If such triangles have their third vertex on the arc of the circle, they are right triangles whose right angle is at the vertex on the arc. He also attempted to establish the height of the Kheops pyramid by using the concept of similar triangles. He measured the length of the shadow of the pyramid on the ground at the moment when his own shadow measured the same as his height. His approximate measure of the pyramid was astonishingly accurate.

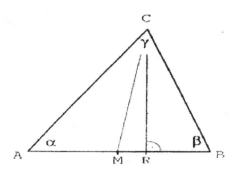

FIGURE 6.1 Triangulation

One of the first actual triangulation efforts was undertaken by another Greek, named Aristarchos in the third century BC. He was also a native of the island of Samos, Pythagoras' birthplace, albeit several centuries later. The wealth of knowledge and talent in the Mediterranean during those times is truly amazing. He was an early proponent of a heliocentric solar system model and there is a crater named after him on the Moon.

He attempted to measure the distance of the Sun from the Earth by measuring one angle of the right triangle formed by the Earth, Sun and the Moon, the latter being the location of the right angle. In fact his work titled *On the sizes and distances of the Sun and the Moon* has survived the millennia to our time. He chose the time when exactly half of the Moon was illuminated by the Sun's rays. Due to the coarse measuring techniques and the fact that the angle he was trying to measure was almost 90 degrees, his results were somewhat crude. Nevertheless, he demonstrated the concept for astronomical measurements.

Extending the trigonometric functions, defined in the right triangle, to general triangles results in relations like the so-called law of sines:

$$\frac{sin(\alpha)}{sin(\beta)} = \frac{\overline{BC}}{\overline{AC}}$$

following the notation in Figure 6.1.

Let us assume that there are two observers located at points A and B, and their distance $\overline{AB}$ is known. They are able to measure the angle between the target point (C) and the other observer point, α and β, respectively. Their goal is, however, to measure the distance of point C from the line AB, but there is an obstacle like a river between them preventing the direct measurement. This means finding the point R on the line AB and that is in general not the same as the mid-point M of the line unless one is extremely lucky. The distance is measured by $\overline{RC}$. Using above law of sines, it follows that

$$\frac{sin(\beta)}{\overline{AC}} = \frac{sin(\gamma)}{\overline{AB}}.$$

The subdivision of the general triangle into two right triangles results in the simple applications of the sine function as

$$\overline{RC} = \overline{AC}sin(\alpha),$$

and
$$\overline{RC} = \overline{BC}sin(\beta).$$
Substituting into the sine law, we obtain
$$\overline{RC} = \overline{AB}\frac{sin(\alpha)sin(\beta)}{sin(\gamma)}.$$
The γ angle of course is not known, but using the fact that the sum of the angles of the triangle is 180 degrees, we can state
$$\gamma = 180 - (\alpha + \beta).$$
We have previously seen the trigonometric relationship of supplementary angles, that here becomes
$$sin(\gamma) = sin(\alpha + \beta)$$
resulting in the formula for the distance as
$$\overline{RC} = \overline{AB}\frac{sin(\alpha)sin(\beta)}{sin(\alpha + \beta)}.$$
Now all the terms on the right hand side are known by measurement enabling the computation of the distance that cannot be measured. The three known quantities are two angles and a distance.

Triangulation is also helpful when not only the distance of a third point is the goal, but when the distance between two inaccessible points is needed. This could be the scenario for example when a surveyor needs to measure the distance between two objects that are across a waterway. This four point triangulation may be accomplished from the lone known distance between the two accessible points and four angles measured from those points. Two of them are the sight angles of the two distant points from each known point. The other two angles are between the line of sight of one of the distant points and the other known point, respectively.

Another triangulation process is used to discretize irregular geometric domains. This triangulation technique is based on the concept originally introduced by the Ukrainian mathematician Voronoi published at the dawn of the 20th century, now called Voronoi polygons. Such a polygon, assigned to a certain point of a set of points on the plane, contains all the points that are closer to the selected point than to any other point of the set.

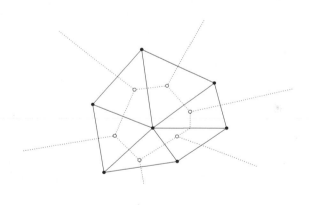

FIGURE 6.2 Delaunay triangulation

In Figure 6.2 the solid dots represent such a set of

points. The irregular (dotted line) hexagon containing one point in the center is the Voronoi polygon of the point in the center. It is easy to see that the points inside the polygon are closer to the center point than to any other points of the set.

The union of the Voronoi polygons of all the points in the set completely covers the plane, meaning that the Voronoi polygons of any two points of the set do not have common interior points, at most they share points on their common boundary.

An extension of the Voronoi concept by his student Delaunay (a Russian but with French ancestry, hence the name) published in the 1930s led to the process now called Delaunay triangulation. The process is based on the Voronoi polygons by constructing edges connecting those points whose Voronoi polygons have a common edge. Constructing all such possible edges will result in the covering of the planar region of our interest with triangular regions, the Delaunay triangles.

The process results in a set of triangles covering the plane as shown in Figure 6.2 with 6 Delaunay triangles where the dotted lines are the edges of the Voronoi polygons and the solid lines depict the Delaunay edges.

Using this process, irregular geometric objects may be covered by triangles enabling the simple description of any physical phenomenon occurring over the region. The triangle, while the simplest of geometric objects, attained immense importance in our lives, but its specific role does not end in geometry. Triangular shapes are very advantageous in certain algebraic operations leading to the concept of triangularization.

Linear systems of equations have been the subject of mathematics for millennia. Simultaneous solution of two equations with two unknowns was known and routinely executed in the middle ages. The solution of the equation system of

$$ax + by = c$$

and

$$dx + ey = f$$

is a standard topic in high school mathematics. Multiplying one equation by an appropriate number then adding the two equations together results in an equation containing only one unknown. The method is applicable to multiple equations with multiple unknowns, but when a system of equations of three unknowns was posed to us as homework in high school, we all cringed. The method is increasingly hard to execute when the number of equations is even larger.

The solution to this problem came from Gauss, another giant of mathematics who also deserves a few biographical words. Johann Gauss was born in the town of Braunschweig, now in Germany, in 1777 and was a child prodigy astonishing his teachers already in elementary school. He completed his work titled *Disquisitiones Arithmeticae* at age 21 and was arguably one of the most prolific mathematicians of all times. He has contributions to almost every area of mathematics: number theory (prime number theorem), analysis (fundamental theorem of algebra), statistics (least squares), differential geometry (Gaussian curvature) and so on.

Gauss devised a method of triangularization of an equation system to reach an easy to solve form. The method is now commonly known as the Gaussian elimination since the triangularization is accomplished by strategically eliminating a block of the non-zero coefficients of the system of equation.

For simplicity of the discussion we discuss the method only with three equations, but all said here applies for any number, even millions of, equations. Let us consider the system of

$$a_{11}x_1 + a_{12}x_2 + a_{13}x_3 = b_1,$$
$$a_{21}x_1 + a_{22}x_2 + a_{23}x_3 = b_2,$$
$$a_{31}x_1 + a_{32}x_2 + a_{33}x_3 = b_3.$$

Gauss' tremendous insight was to devise a process to reduce the general system to a system whose shape is triangular by capturing the original idea from the middle ages. He proposed executing systematic multiplication and addition of equations until the shape of the system became triangular:

$$\bar{a}_{11}x_1 + \bar{a}_{12}x_2 + \bar{a}_{13}x_3 = \bar{b}_1,$$
$$\bar{a}_{22}x_2 + \bar{a}_{23}x_3 = \bar{b}_2,$$
$$\bar{a}_{33}x_3 = \bar{b}_3.$$

The coefficients of the system of course undergo some change during the triangularization process, denoted by the bar over the terms, but the resulting advantage is spectacular. The solution of this triangular system of equations now may be accomplished by a simple so-called back-substitution reflecting the fact that the solutions of the system are obtained in a backward order. First the last equation may easily be solved for the lone unknown of x_3 as

$$x_3 = \frac{\overline{b}_3}{\overline{a}_{33}}.$$

Then the previous to last equation is solved by utilizing the already known solution value of x_3 to solve for the lone unknown x_2:

$$x_2 = \frac{\overline{b}_2 - \overline{a}_{23}x_3}{\overline{a}_{22}}.$$

The process continues repeating the same steps with increasingly larger number of known terms until the very first equation is solved as

$$x_1 = \frac{\overline{b}_1 - \overline{a}_{12}x_2 - \overline{a}_{13}x_3}{\overline{a}_{11}}.$$

The triangularization and the follow-up back substitution processes are clearly generalizable to larger size problems because the triangular shape can be extended indefinitely while still maintaining the process.

The intrinsic importance of the systematic method is obvious when one considers the possibility of computer execution of the process for very large systems of equations consisting of millions of equations. The process lends itself to computer implementation very easily. The recursive execution of repeated computational patterns is extremely tedious for humans, but it is the forte of computers.

The coefficients of such large systems are used to describe the physical behavior of some mechanical object, an airplane, a car or a ship. The right hand side of the system describes some physical loads applied to the object, forces of nature, vibrations induced by the road or the ocean's waves. Another manifestation of the immense practicality of the simple triangle, the geometric messenger of the number three.

7

Three dimensional universe

We are living in a three dimensional universe, as far as we perceive it. The three dimensional nature of our (at least geometric) universe is well demonstrated by the fact of how the interstellar probes we send to some other planets of our solar system navigate. They certainly cannot do that with the help of the earthly concept of the compass and the magnetic north. Spacecraft locations are pinpointed in a three dimensional coordinate system with very specific reference to Earth.

This coordinate system is centered at the Earth and has a "horizontal" plane defined by the mean equatorial plane. This plane is specified by removing the wobbling of the Earth's axis and the resulting change of the plane.

The vertical axis of the system is defined by the line drawn from the Earth to the Sun on the first day of spring. There is also a reference time defined as January 1, 2000 in order to account for and adjust to the changes in the reference plane caused by the gravitational forces of the other planets in the solar system.

The location of any spacecraft may be firmly established in this coordinate system, most commonly by the astronomical technique of using two angles. They are the right ascension that is an angle measure in the "horizontal" plane, and the declination that is the angle above or below the plane. With the addition of a measure of the distance of the spacecraft, the triple (two angles and the distance) becomes what is known as a spherical coordinate system. This system of the three quantities describes locations not just inside our solar system, but in our galaxy as well.

The first three dimensional objects investigated by the ancient geometers were various polyhedra; objects bounded by planes, defined by edges and vertices. The most important and first historically, shown in Figure 7.1, is the tetrahedron. It is really an extension of the fundamental planar building block of the triangle into three dimensions. All four of its sides are triangles and their practical importance will become clear later.

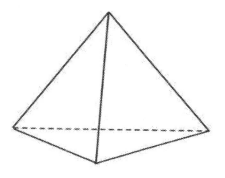

FIGURE 7.1 Tetrahedron

There is a special class of three dimensional geometric objects, called regular polyhedra, and three occupies a special role in their construction. Regular polyhedra are objects whose sides are regular polygons consisting of equal sides and angles. They are sometimes known as Platonic solids, named after another Greek philosopher, Plato who lived in the 5th century BC.

Plato's birth place is not known, but it is assumed to be in or near Athens. He was of a privileged upbringing in a noble family and received superior education. He founded the Academy in Athens and one of his students was Aristotle, mentioned in an earlier chapter. While not mainly known for his mathematical work, he was intrigued by these solid objects and contributed to an early classification of them, hence the name.

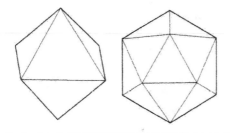

FIGURE 7.2 Octahedron and icosahedron

There are five of these regular polyhedra: the above tetrahedron, the hexahedron, the octahedron, the dodecahedron with 12 faces and the icosahedron with 20 faces. Three of the regular polyhedra, the tetrahedron, as well as the octahedron and the icosahedron, shown in Figure 7.2, have triangular faces. The octahedron as its name indicates has eight triangular faces that are all the same shape. The icosahedron is built from twenty triangles and is the most complex, but extremely beautiful, regular solid.

Three of them, the tetrahedron of Figure 7.1, the hexahedron and the dodecahedron, shown in Figure 7.3, have vertices where three faces meet. The hexahedron has six quadrilateral faces and the dodecahedron has twelve pentagonal faces.

There were some curious beliefs about the regular solids. Some considered the five regular solids to be representing our universe. The external layer was supposed to be a tetrahedron containing a cube inside. Inside the cube was an octahedron that in turn contained a dodecahedron. The innermost object was an icosahedron, the most complex one of all, representing our world.

Our algebraic representation of the three dimensional geometric world is in the familiar Cartesian coordinate system where each point is represented by three coordinates

$$P = (x, y, z).$$

This extremely convenient representation is credited to the French mathematician and philosopher, Descartes

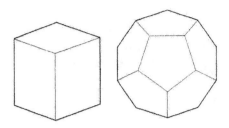

FIGURE 7.3 Hexahedron and dodecahedron

of the early 17th century, who is famous for his phrase of "cogito, ergo sum". The system enables us to manipulate difficult three dimensional objects in simple algebraic terms, technically called analytic geometry. Long gone is the geometric construction of the two dimensional flatlands. We are dealing with objects in space. Any two points in the three dimensional space also define a line. The generalization of Pythagorean theorem to three dimensions results in the distance between two points as

$$d^2 = (x_2 - x_1)^2 + (y_2 - y_1)^2 + (z_2 - z_1)^2.$$

Furthermore any three points define a plane by specifying three lines between any two points of the three, hence a triangle. Carrying further, four points in the three dimensional space not located on the same plane define three distinct planes and a volume bordered by four triangles, i.e. the tetrahedron. As triangles are used to fill out an irregular two dimensional geometric shape, tetrahedra may be used to fill up a three dimensional volume.

Trigonometry, whose powers were explained in detail in Chapter 5, may be generalized into three dimensions. Retaining the triangles' planar shape, but allowing various triangles to be located in different planes of the three dimensional coordinate system results in a wealth of possibilities.

The very simple triangulation concept for distance measurement introduced in Chapter 6 is easily generalized such a way and it is widely used in astronomy to measure the distance and size of very far objects based on known distances and measurable angles. This process is especially powerful when used recursively. Once the distance of an inaccessible point is known, and most objects in the sky are inaccessible to us, its distance may be used as a known point in furthering the triangulation.

The global positioning system (GPS) devices also solve a three dimensional triangulation problem to find the location of a point with respect to three known points that are in various positions in the sky, as depicted in Figure 7.4. They measure the distances between the location of the receiver and three satellites orbiting Earth orbit by sending and receiving an electromagnetic signal.

The relative position of the satellites defined by their distances to each other and to the receiver allow to pinpoint the location of the receiver on Earth with

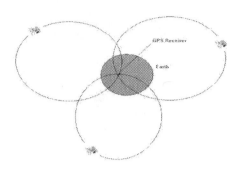

FIGURE 7.4 GPS triangulation

extreme accuracy. A little trigonometry is all that is needed. The concept will not work with less than three satellites but does not need any more than three satellites, the magic of three is at work again.

The other triangulation process of tiling irregular domains shown in the last chapter may also be generalized to three dimensions and it is called Delaunay tessellation. In three dimensions the Voronoi polygon becomes a polyhedron containing all points closer to a point in three dimensions. Since each point in space is surrounded by four such polyhedra, the Delaunay triangles become tetrahedra. As a result of this process, a three dimensional object so discretized will be comprised of tetrahedra in the interior and covered by triangles (the sides of the tetrahedra) on the surface.

This tessellation process is widely applied for irregu-

lar three dimensional objects in sciences, ranging from
physical to biological sciences. Even human body parts,
admittedly irregularly shaped objects, are discretized
by tetrahedra based tessellation. An example of tessellation is shown in Figure 7.5 where a human hand
model is discretized into tetrahedra. The process results in the hand's exterior surface being covered with
triangles. Due to the coarse level of discretization, the
shape appears to be crude, but that is easily overcome
by further refinement.

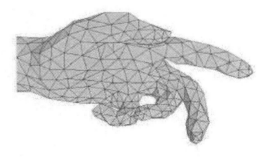

FIGURE 7.5 Tessellation of a hand

The fact that the exterior surface of a tessellated volume becomes tiled with triangles is utilized for computer graphics purposes in the computer game and
film industry. Even if the object may be described
by more accurate means, the speed of displaying the

planar triangular shapes is much faster than displaying the accurate geometry, making the techniques attractive. With large number of tetrahedra, and in turn triangles on the surface, the image is accurate enough, but the sizes of the tetrahedra resulting in the triangles may also be refined as necessary to be acceptable by human eyes.

To be truthful about the dimensionality of our universe, we should mention the name Minkowski. He was born in the second half of the 19th century in an area of modern day Lithuania, then part of the Russian empire. He worked most of his mathematical life in Germany and Switzerland. While in Switzerland, he was briefly the teacher of Einstein and their work also remains connected forever. Minkowski proposed a four dimensional physical space comprised of the three geometric dimensions augmented by time as the fourth dimension. In this space the distance between two points was defined as

$$d^2 = c^2(t_2 - t_1)^2 - (x_2 - x_1)^2 - (y_2 - y_1)^2 - (z_2 - z_1)^2$$

with the t denoting time and c the speed of light. In some sense the three dimensional spherical system, described in the beginning of this chapter for the motion of extraterrestrial objects, already had a hidden time component in the reference time that was used to fix the "vertical" axis of the system. It appears that once we step outside Earth, we are in a four dimensional space.

Minkowski's four dimensional space, published in the first decade of the 20th century, fit perfectly into Einstein's special relativity theory, in fact it resolved some of its mathematical difficulties. The resulting relativistic space-time continuum of the physical universe is now widely accepted by scientists to be the way things work on the astronomical scale. The lack of our ability to reconcile this theory with the world of the small in the realm of particle physics is one of the grand challenges of our times.

There are new attempts, some rather esoteric, like the string theory. It proposes that the universe is of eleven dimensions in which the strings apparently live and provide the foundation of our existence. A string is supposedly a one dimensional object in this eleven dimensional space, much like a curve in our three dimensions. Then there are intermediate, more than one, but less than eleven dimensional objects called 2, 3, 4, ...-branes. They are just like membranes (hence the name) are two dimensional objects in our three-space. The theory is highly contested, entirely unproven and mostly unexplained.

With all honesty, we must admit: three geometric dimensions and one tentative step beyond it into time is all we can reach at the moment, another gateway role of the number three.

8

Primal three and the ongoing quest

The number three is a member of an exclusive class of numbers, the prime numbers. Such numbers can only be divided by one and themselves to yield a whole number and they are something of an enigma. We still do not know a rule of how to generate a sequence of such numbers or describe their distribution on the number line. Three is somewhat special by its location at the onset of the list of primes.

It is the very first of regular primes and it is an odd prime as are all of the prime numbers apart from the even 2. There is no other even prime number, since any other even number may be divided by two thus violating the definition. Some consider one and two as being irregular primes. Even more do not consider one being a prime at all, albeit it certainly satisfies the literal definition.

All the other numbers that are not prime numbers are called composite numbers since they can be factored by a number other than 1 and themselves. For example, the number 4, the first composite number, may be constructed as the product of 1 and 4, either as 1 times 4 or 4 times 1. On the other hand, it may also be composed as 2 times 2, which is a composition that disqualifies it from being a prime. Hence, prime numbers are the ultimate building blocks of our number world. Every non-prime could be composed of primes, but primes cannot be composed of other numbers. They are indivisible.

The very first occurrence of prime numbers appears to be in Euclid's work about 300 BC or thereabouts. In fact, Euclid already proved that there are infinite number of prime numbers, possibly initiating the biggest conundrum of counting; the fact that there are several sets of numbers that coexist on the number line and all contain infinite number of members. This conundrum was ultimately resolved by the Russia born German mathematician Cantor only in the end of the 19th century with his famous counting principles, a subject of a later chapter.

Euclid's ingenious proof is conceptually rather simple. He said: let us assume that the number of primes is finite. Then we could gather all the prime numbers together and multiply them. Then let us add one to the product and consider the two possibilities that we obtained either a new prime number or a composite number. If it is a prime number then obviously the original set did not contain all the prime numbers and the starting assumption that there is a finite number of primes was incorrect.

On the other hand, if the new number generated is a composite number then it must have a factor that is not part of the original set of primes. Hence another prime must be present outside of the finite list of all the primes. Clearly, both scenarios indicate that there is an infinite number of primes, as one can always generate another prime, no matter how large the set is.

It follows from the above logic that the number of composite numbers is infinite as well. After all, every new prime number generated by the above process could be used to generate an infinite number of new composite numbers. This is easy to see if we consider that every prime number, for example our favorite the number 3, can generate an infinite number of new composite numbers as $3 \cdot 3 = 9, 3 \cdot 3 \cdot 3 = 27, 3 \cdot 3 \cdot 3 \cdot 3 = 81, \ldots, 3 \cdot 3 \ldots \cdot 3 = 3^k$, where k is the number of multiplications by 3. This could be done infinite number of times, hence we can generate infinite number of new composite numbers from each new prime.

The simple definition of prime numbers lulls us into believing that the process of generating prime numbers is easy. Sure enough, the Greek Eratosthenes devised a scheme of finding prime numbers sometime around 200 BC. Eratosthenes also lived in Alexandria, like Euclid, but three quarters of a century later. He attempted to measure the size of the Earth, a very ambitious attempt considering the time and the tools available to him. His scheme to find prime numbers, while conceptually very simple but extremely tedious, relied on listing all the numbers up to a certain number and successively crossing out the multiples of already established primes. The process, called Eratosthenes' sieve, worked by dropping every second number after 2, then every third number after 3, then every fifth after 5 and so on.

For example finding the primes up to 15 may be accomplished by the method as follows:

$$1, 2, 3, 4, 5, 6, 7, 8, 9, 10, 11, 12, 13, 14, 15,$$

$$1, 2, 3, x, 5, x, 7, x, 9, x, 11, x, 13, x, 15,$$

$$1, 2, 3, x, 5, x, 7, x, x, x, 11, x, 13, x, x.$$

The dropping of every fifth number would be the next in the process, but 10 is already dropped because of being a multiple of 2, and 15 is already dropped because it is a multiple of 3. Dropping every seventh number would require us to drop 14 but it is already dropped as a multiple of 2. Since the 11 is the next remaining number, its first drop of 22 is outside of the range of our interest, hence the process is stopped. The primes of the range 1 to 15 are $1, 2, 3, 5, 7, 11, 13$.

It is also interesting to recognize a pattern in the form of the first few primes:

$$2^2 - 1 = 3, \ 2^2 + 1 = 5$$

both are primes, while

$$2^3 - 1 = 7, \ 2^3 + 1 = 9$$

is a pair of a prime and a composite number. Then

$$2^4 - 1 = 15, \ 2^4 + 1 = 17$$

is a composite-prime pair. Some of the $2^k \pm 1$ forms will produce primes as visible in our examples above, but not all.

The French amateur mathematician Fermat, a lawyer by training, conjectured in the 17th century that when the exponent is a power of 2, the numbers of the form

$$2^{2^n} + 1,$$

will be primes. Such numbers are nowadays called Fermat numbers. Our number 3 is the first Fermat number since $3 = 2^{2^0} + 1$. It is also a prime. However, not all the Fermat numbers turned out to be primes, contrary to Fermat's belief.

The Fermat numbers that correspond to the exponents

$$n = 0, 1, 2, 3, 4,$$

resulting in

$$3, 5, 17, 257, 65537,$$

turned out to be primes. A century after Fermat, however, the Swiss mathematician Leonhard Euler, another giant of mathematics, proved that $2^{2^5} + 1$ is not a prime. With the advent of computer technology many large Fermat numbers were tested, up to the tens of thousands of the value of n, the power of two in the exponent, and they all were found to be composite. It is still an open question whether the first five Fermat numbers up to $n = 4$ are the only primes of this class.

A very intriguing relationship was proven in the 1800s by Gauss, stating that the prime Fermat numbers correspond to the only regular polygons with prime number of sides that may be constructed by a straight edge and a compass. We know we can construct a triangle and a pentagon, but why can't we construct a septagon? The proof required the mind of Gauss and is well beyond our focus here, but we are left to wonder why this is true.

The primal nature of 3 is more than simply being the first regular prime, or the first Fermat number. It is also a member of other classes of prime definitions. For example, it is also the first so-called Mersenne prime, that is, primes of form $2^p - 1$ where p is a prime number. This class was invented by Mersenne, a French monk in the early 1600s, who was incidentally a classmate of Descartes of the coordinate system fame.

Clearly $2^2 - 1 = 3$ is the first prime of this form and the next number, $2^3 - 1 = 7$ is another member. The next few Mersenne primes, $2^5 - 1 = 31$, and $2^7 - 1 = 127$ were already discovered as primes by the ancient Greeks. Several of the Mersenne primes, like $2^{17} - 1$ and $2^{19} - 1$ were discovered as primes by others in the middle ages, before Mersenne's classification. The first big prime discovered as a Mersenne prime was $2^{31} - 1$ by Euler in the 18th century.

The class of Mersenne numbers, however, is still not an all encompassing class. For example, $2^p - 1$ is not a prime for $p = 11, 23, 29, 37$. Nevertheless, this is an efficient definition for establishing new primes, even in the age of the most advanced computers. In order to accelerate the search for Mersenne primes we can turn to another interesting facet of the three, the so-called three member sequence, a subject of more discussion in a later chapter.

The French Lucas in the middle of the 19th century proposed a sequence of

$$L_k = L_{k-1} + L_{k-2},$$

starting from the terms

$$L_0 = 2$$

and
$$L_1 = 1$$

Then

$$L_2 = 2 + 1 = 3,$$

and so on. The sequence, that is now known as the Lucas sequence, then becomes

$$L_k = 2, 1, 3, 4, 7, 11, 18, 29, 47 \ldots.$$

The interesting result is that many of the Lucas numbers, as the members of this sequence are known, are primes. In fact, except for the cases of 4 and 18 above the others are all primes (overlooking the ambiguity about the prime-ness of one and two) Since the Lucas numbers are very easy to generate via the definition of the sequence, they provide an efficient way in computational number theory to search for very large prime numbers, the subject of the ongoing quest.

Another specific role of the number 3 in the prime number world arises from the fact that it is the only prime adjacent to another prime, i.e. to 2. Hence many primes are of the form

$$(2 \cdot 3)n \pm 1,$$

where n is an integer. For example, $n = 1$ gives rise to 5 and 7, $n = 2$ to 11 and 13, $n = 3$ to 17 and 19. However, $n = 4$ and $n = 6$ do not produce primes, but $n = 5$ and $n = 7$ produce $29, 31$ and $41, 43$ respectively. This might lead us to believe that primes are of the form

$$(2 \cdot 3)p \pm 1,$$

where p is a prime. The $p = 11$ case, however, shatters our hopes, since 65 is not a prime. As is the case with many of the promising prime number hypotheses, this proves to be invalid as well, but nevertheless provides another interesting insight.

Let us organize the natural numbers in two groups of three terms in a row as

$$
\begin{array}{ccccccc}
\mathbf{1}, & \mathbf{2}, & \mathbf{3}, & 4, & \mathbf{5}, & 6 \\
\mathbf{7}, & 8, & 9, & 10, & \mathbf{11}, & 12 \\
\mathbf{13}, & 14, & 15, & 16, & \mathbf{17}, & 18 \\
\mathbf{19}, & 20, & 21, & 22, & \mathbf{23}, & 24 \\
25, & 26, & 27, & 28, & \mathbf{29}, & 30 \\
\mathbf{31}, & 32, & 33, & 34, & 35, & 36 \\
\mathbf{37}, & 38, & 39, & 40, & \mathbf{41}, & 42 \\
\mathbf{43}, & 44, & 45, & 46, & \mathbf{47}, & 48
\end{array}
$$

Observing the locations of the primes denoted by the bold numbers above, it is noticeable that after the first, initialization row, there is only one column in the two triple column arrangements that contains primes. The first column of the first triple and the second column of the second triple (a wonderful symmetry there). The other columns do not contain primes at all. Unfortunately not all the numbers in the two prime containing columns are primes, the first column breaks the pattern at 25, the second column at 35. Therefore this is not the panacea humankind is looking for, and the location of prime numbers remains the subject of an ongoing quest.

There is a beguiling conjecture by the German mathematician Goldbach stating that every even number above 3 (a gateway again) may be written as the sum of two primes. Clearly,

$$4 = 2 + 2, \; 6 = 3 + 3, \; 8 = 3 + 5, \ldots$$

Some even numbers even have two such sums. For example

$$10 = 3 + 7 = 5 + 5.$$

The conjecture is still unproven after some 250 years. It is, however, even more remarkable that it has not been disproved either despite modern computer aided searches up the order of 10^{10}. This fact lands credibility to the conjecture, but of course does not guarantee it to be true.

There is an ongoing deep human fascination with large primes. The presently known largest prime was found in 2008 by a group of researchers and it is the Mersenne prime

$$2^{43112609} - 1.$$

The number is comprised of 12,978,189 digits, and is the 45th known Mersenne prime. Such numbers are searched as much for trying to establish a pattern of their distribution as for trying to glimpse into another one of universe's secrets.

Why would this topic be so important? It is, because knowing the location of prime numbers in general would enable factoring very large numbers with ease. This would place the encryption systems of the financial world in jeopardy, as the secret codes used for transactions may be easily deciphered. This is a very powerful incentive to continue the quest, not to mention the potential immortality of the person actually achieving the solution of a problem that humbled many genius mathematicians in the past centuries.

9

French obsession with the power three

Insofar we mainly focused on the powerful roles of the number three. Let us now investigate the power of three in the mathematical sense. From the very first years of mathematical thinking, people were challenged by the intricacies of raising a number to the third power. They were especially interested in finding the relationship between cubic (numbers that are the third power of another number) and other natural numbers. Ancient Greek mathematicians had already discovered that cubic numbers can always be written as the sum of successive odd numbers. Clearly the progression

$$1^3 = 1$$

$$2^3 = 3 + 5 = 8,$$

$$3^3 = 7 + 9 + 11 = 27,$$

and so on demonstrates that. A larger example may be

$$5^3 = 21 + 23 + 25 + 27 + 29 = 125,$$

indicating that the rule is generic. It is actually rather easy to generate such a number sequence for any cubic number by observing that even cubic numbers are composed by an even number of successive odd numbers. On the converse, an odd cubic number is composed of an odd number of successive odd numbers and the number of the components is the same as the base of the cubic number, e.g. two for $8 = 2^3$ and five for $125 = 5^3$.

A more intriguing question was the opposite of the above, namely, how can any natural number be represented by summing up cubic numbers? This is something entirely different. Let us view a cubic number first. It is represented naturally by one single cube, for example $27 = 3^3$. On the other hand, let us consider a non-cubic number, for example 23.

$$23 = 2^3 + 2^3 + 1^3 + 1^3 + 1^3 + 1^3 + 1^3 + 1^3 + 1^3.$$

This required the sum of nine (3^3) cubes. A lesser known English mathematician, Waring, conjectured in the 18th century that every natural number can be produced as the sum of at most nine cubes. This would be certainly true for all cubic numbers, but for example

$$36 = 3^3 + 2^3 + 1^3,$$

required only three cubes. The importance of Waring's theorem is that no matter how large the number becomes, the number of cubes to sum will not grow beyond nine. It required about two more centuries to prove that the only other number besides 23 that actually requires nine cubes to sum is 239 which may be written as

$$239 = 4^3 + 4^3 + 3^3 + 3^3 + 3^3 + 3^3 + 1^3 + 1^3 + 1^3.$$

This is an extremely curious fact that seems to imply that even very large numbers can be the sum of at most eight cubes. The fundamental, gateway nature of 3 is glaring in our eyes again and we are at a loss for an explanation.

As curious as that fact is, it is even more interesting that at the moment the largest number that requires the sum of eight cubes appears to be only 454. This was established with the help of computers that systematically searched for such numbers up to $50,000$. The search continues, but it appears to hint at a maximum number above which all numbers may be the sum of less than eight cubes.

The Greek Diophantus around 100 BC attempted to find solutions for equations of the following type

$$x^3 + y^3 = z^3.$$

He also worked in Alexandria as did Euclid and Eratosthenes, and wrote a text titled *Arithmetica*, that survived the times. As Euclid is now called the father of geometry, Diophantus is called the father of algebra. He found that the quadratic case of the problem is easily solvable if we assume that the numbers are of the form

$$x = a + \sqrt{2ab},$$

and

$$y = b + \sqrt{2ab},$$

where $2ab$ is a perfect square, so its square root produces an integer. Then using the well known binomial formula produces

$$x^2 + y^2 = a^2 + 2a\sqrt{2ab} + 2ab + b^2 + 2b\sqrt{2ab} + 2ab.$$

Reordering and grouping the right hand side results in

$$(a+b)^2 + 2(a+b)\sqrt{2ab} + 2ab = (a+b+\sqrt{2ab})^2 = z^2.$$

Hence the third integer will be of form

$$z = a + b + \sqrt{2ab}.$$

The process of generating Pythagorean triples based on this is very easy. Let us choose for example $x = 5$. We need to write 5 as the sum of a number a and a root of a perfect square. This is possible in only one way,

$$x = 5 = 1 + 4.$$

Hence we have $a = 1$ and since

$$4 = \sqrt{2ab} = \sqrt{2 \cdot 1 \cdot b} = \sqrt{2 \cdot 1 \cdot 8} = \sqrt{16}.$$

we get $b = 8$ and

$$y = 8 + \sqrt{2ab} = 8 + 4 = 12.$$

Therefore,

$$z = 1 + 8 + \sqrt{16} = 13$$

and surely

$$5^2 + 12^2 = 13^2$$

holds true. To alleviate any suspicion arising from the omission of the case of $x = 4$, let us follow the same process

$$x = 4 = 2 + \sqrt{4} = 2 + \sqrt{2 \cdot 2 \cdot 1},$$

resulting in $b = 1, y = 1 + \sqrt{4} = 3$ and $z = 2 + 1 + 2 = 5$. This is the already discussed Pythagorean triple, so the process properly functions independently of whether $x > y$ or vice versa.

It also works for cases when the starting number x is producible in more than one way. For example,

$$x = 9 = 1 + 8 = 5 + 4$$

are both proper forms. The first case would result in $y = 12$ and $z = 15$; the second pairing in $y = 40$ and $z = 41$. Clearly both

$$9^2 + 12^2 = 15^2$$

and

$$9^2 + 40^2 = 41^2$$

are valid. Diophantus gave a lot of attention to the cubic problem but was unable to find a solution for that case. For almost 1700 years after him, mathematicians were either trying to solve the problem or prove that it is unsolvable.

Fermat, the aforementioned amateur mathematician, lawyer by training, during the 1600s stated something intriguing that initiated an obsession with mathematicians for centuries to come. He stated on the margin of Diophantus' book *Arithmetica* that the reason Diophantus was unable to solve the cubic problem was because it is impossible to solve the equation

$$x^n + y^n = z^n$$

for any $n > 2$ with whole numbers. He also wrote that he can prove it, but the margin does not have enough

space to contain the proof. Since all of his other theorems were proved either by him or some other mathematicians, except for this one, it became known as
Fermat's last theorem.

For a while hopes were focused on finding a counterexample demonstrating the fallacy of Fermat's conjecture. They were some very close calls in that regard.
Several examples were found like

$$6^3 + 18^3 = 9^3 - 1,$$

or

$$216 + 512 = 729 - 1,$$

where the discrepancy was only one. But none exactly disproving the conjecture was even found. Fermat himself proved the $n = 4$ case indirectly, when
working on another problem. The method he employed was what we call today the method of infinite
descent. Fermat aimed at a contradiction by assuming
that the problem has a solution, for example

$$x_1^4 + y_1^4 = z_1^4.$$

From this assumption he was able to show that then
there must be another, smaller, solution, say x_2, y_2, z_2
to the problem. Applying the same argument repeatedly results in an infinitely continuing smaller and
smaller solution triple. This, however, contradicts the
the fact that the solution numbers must be natural
numbers that implies a smallest solution set. Hence
the original assumption of having any solution is false,
there is no natural number solution to

$$x^4 + y^4 = z^4.$$

Finally, Euler in the 17th century proved that there is
no natural number solution to the power three problem of the form

$$x^3 + y^3 = z^3$$

either. This was especially important, since 3 is a
prime (an illustrious one) and if one could prove that
the theorem holds for all primes, that would imply to
hold for all composite numbers, hence for all numbers,
as well.

Another hundred years or so passed by before the
French Dirichlet proved that the power 5 case of

$$x^5 + y^5 = z^5$$

has no integer solution either. Another French mathematician, Lame proved the case for the third prime,
$n = 7$ in the 1830s. His solution was in part based
on the work of the also French Sophie Germain. She
was one of the first woman mathematicians at a time
when such an activity was frowned upon when done
by a lady. She overcame this stigma by presenting her
work under the alias of a man and was successful in
holding up a correspondence even with Gauss.

Sophie Germain in the early 1800s investigated numbers of the form

$$2 \cdot p + 1,$$

where p is a prime. She noticed that such numbers are
often also primes, in fact they are now called Germain
primes to her honor. This class of numbers became
instrumental in proving the $n = 7$ case of Fermat's

conjecture.

By that time the topic became a French national obsession to the extent that the French Academy of Sciences in 1850 announced a grand price of 3,000 Francs for the solution of the problem. About a dozen mathematicians presented solutions that hoped to prove or disprove the conjecture. The most famous was Cauchy who in one of the Academy meetings even announced to have a solution, to be proven faulty later along with all the others.

The quest continued almost until the end of the millennium. The general case for any power was finally proven only in the last decade of the 20th century by a British mathematician Andrew Wiles, working in the United States. He presented his proof in 1995, the result of a lifetime of fascination and a decade of dedicated research of the topic. The proof cannot be presented by common mathematical means and would require a volume of the size of this book to describe. It was certainly an understatement by Fermat that the margin was too small to show his proof of the general theorem.

We will leave it at the level that it is proven and duly note another gateway manifestation of the number 3. It is, of course, a closed gateway marking the boundary of something that cannot be done, starting from 3.

To demonstrate a truly practical power of three, let us point to its astonishing presence in the ancient art of shipbuilding. It is well known that thousands of years ago various nations in the Mediterranean built complex ships with intricately curved ribs bent from natural wood beams. It turns out that the geometric shapes of those ribs where what we call today piecewise cubic curves. What that means is that the sections between the supports of the ribs where simple cubic polynomials, algebraic expressions of the form

$$y(x) = a_1 + a_2 x + a_3 x^2 + a_4 x^3.$$

The mathematical reason for this is rooted in the fact that the physical phenomenon of the bending of a flexible beam into the shape by straight (tangential) constraints is described by a differential equation whose analytic solution is in the form of cubic polynomials.

Incidentally the methodology spread into the modern shipbuilding industry where the lines of the ship profile were laid out on the floor with flexible wooden rulers, called splines. The flexible rulers, made from teak wood, were held in place by lead weights enforcing the ruler to be stationary at certain points and holding a certain direction, thereby influencing the shape. The lead weights were called dolphins and clearly we are long beyond the straight edge here.

The example curve shown in Figure 9.1 is comprised of three segments specified by four points and the tangents at those points. The complete curve is beautifully shaped and continuous, just like the wooden ruler bent into the shape of the ship profile. The shapes so obtained were cut into wooden planks of the various cross sections of the ships and in turn those wooden formats were used in the manufacturing to cut the metal rib and longitudinal profiles.

FIGURE 9.1 Spline curve

The mathematical representation of these functions enabled them to seep into many segments of engineering. They are still called splines from their origins in the the naval architect field. They are, however, now used in the mathematical description of very complex curves of nature in our everyday lives; ranging from the shape of our bodies and faces, through those of animals and plants, to the mechanical components of automobiles and household appliances.

This simple building block became indispensable in the computer aided design and manufacturing industries providing another testimonial to the power of three.

10

Italian attack on the cubic barrier

Cubic equations are obtained by equating an algebraic expression involving the power of three with zero and seeking the values of the unknown x that satisfy the condition. Their general form is

$$x^3 + a_1 x^2 + a_2 x + a_3 = 0,$$

where the fact that the coefficient of the cubic term was chosen to be one does not restrict the generality as it can always be achieved by dividing the whole equation with the coefficient of the cubic term.

These equations have challenged humanity for a very long time. While the general solution of quadratic equations was known several centuries BC, the solution of the cubic eluded mankind for almost two millennia. There were some successful attempts to solve certain special types of third degree equations with given integer coefficients.

The stubborn reluctance of the third degree equation to allow a general algebraic solution for unspecified coefficients, however, resulted in a belief in the middle ages that the cubic is an impenetrable barrier. This, however, changed in the early 1500s when the Italian del Ferro was able to solve a specific form of the cubic equation

$$x^3 + px = q,$$

with unspecified coefficients and by purely algebraic means. He restricted the coefficients to be positive numbers, but as it turned out later it was not a necessity. The ingenious idea of del Ferro was to seek the solution in the form of the sum of two components. Substitution into his original third degree equation resulted in a first rather daunting sixth degree equation in a new variable u. It seemed like his idea was wrong. Closer inspection, however, revealed that this was really a quadratic equation in terms of u^3 which of course had a known solution for millennia. Since Del Ferro restricted the coefficients to be positive, the solution was always real. Indeed, by means of calculus one can prove that del Ferro's equation with the positive coefficients will always have a real root.

The saga of the third degree equation continued with another Italian, Tartaglia (a nickname meaning the stammerer), a contemporary of del Ferro, who solved another special form of the cubic:

$$x^3 + rx^2 = q.$$

Neither Tartaglia, not del Ferro figured out a way to solve general problem. The honor of finding that went to a third (!) Italian, Cardano, who according to some sources was really only combining the results of his two predecessors. Some even view him as a plagiarist who just combined and publicized his contemporaries' results into the solution of the general cubic equation.

The solution of the general third degree equation now known as Cardano's formula is

$$x = \sqrt[3]{\frac{q}{2} + \sqrt{\frac{q^2}{4} + \frac{p^3}{27}}} + \sqrt[3]{\frac{q}{2} - \sqrt{\frac{q^2}{4} + \frac{p^3}{27}}} - \frac{a_1}{3}.$$

Here the substitutions are

$$p = (a_2 - \frac{a_1^2}{3})$$

and

$$q = -\frac{2a_1^3}{27} + \frac{a_1 a_2}{3} - a_3.$$

This substitution recasts the general problem as del Ferro's specific problem. Cardano's solution in essence is nothing else but del Ferro's solution without the positive coefficient restriction of del Ferro's. In this case the solution may result in negative numbers under the square root, a fact that puzzled those in the middle ages working on the cubic problem as imaginary numbers were not invented yet. Cardano in fact decided that those cases when the formula ends up with negative square roots are "irreducible cubics" (his name) and just ignored them.

Enter another Italian, a contemporary of Cardano named Bombelli, an engineer. He made the tremendous recognition, that despite the presence of negative numbers under the square root, the sum of the two terms yields a real number. He had boldly decided that one can still solve the problem by assuming that the square roots with negative numbers make sense. Let us denote the troublesome term as

$$s = \frac{q^2}{4} + \frac{p^3}{27}.$$

With that the solution components of Cardano's equation become

$$u = \sqrt[3]{\frac{q}{2} + \sqrt{-s}},$$

and

$$v = \sqrt[3]{\frac{q}{2} - \sqrt{-s}}.$$

Bombelli's trick was as follows. He wrote

$$u^3 + v^3 = \frac{q}{2} + \sqrt{-s} + \frac{q}{2} - \sqrt{-s} = q.$$

Applying the cubic binomial expression

$$(u+v)^3 = u^3 + 3u^2v + 6uv + 3uv^2 + v^3$$

and executing some tedious algebra enabled him to solve for

$$u + v = r.$$

where r was a real number. For example if a cubic equation were to yield

$$\sqrt[3]{10 + \sqrt{-243}} + \sqrt[3]{10 - \sqrt{-243}} = u + v,$$

then Bombelli would write

$$u^3 + v^3 = 10 + \sqrt{-243} + 10 - \sqrt{-243} = 20,$$

and with his tricky algebra obtain the result of

$$u + v = 5.$$

This is very easy to compute with a simple calculator today, but Bombelli certainly did not have one. He also recognized that in the case when Cardano's formula turns out the troublesome negative term under the square root, the cubic equation always has three real solutions. This was probably the most insightful contribution to the topic of the cubic that was really an Italian joint venture.

It appeared that the topic of the cubic was finally put to rest. The fact, however, that the third degree equation was so hard to crack instigated investigations into higher degree algebraic equations. Soon the idea emerged that there is a limit after all, beyond which algebraic equations will not have a closed form solution. Was three the gateway number, albeit open, and no solutions beyond existed?

The fourth order, quartic equation

$$x^4 + a_3x^3 + a_2x^2 + a_1x + a_0 = 0,$$

therefore was also subject of close attention in the Italian mathematical scene. It was brilliantly solved by Ferrari, a contemporary of Cardano, who transformed the quartic equation into a cubic equation, now called the cubic resolvent, that of course was solvable by Cardano's formula. Therefore, he broke through a barrier, solved the quartic by the help of the cubic.

The fifth order, quintic equation

$$x^5 + a_4x^4 + a_3x^3 + a_2x^2 + a_1x + a_0 = 0,$$

however, became a tough nut to crack. The topic endured several centuries of attacks, unbending. Another Italian born mathematician, Lagrange, a native of Turin, picked up the fight in the last quarter

of the 18th century. He analyzed the contributions
of his countrymen and recognized that his predecessors solved the equations by transforming them into a
somewhat simpler form. He also noted that the simpler equation to solve turned out to be a degree lower
than the original, like Ferrari's solution of the quartic
with the help of the cubic.

He was, however, unable to create a quartic auxiliary equation for the quintic. The auxiliary equation
turned out to be not one degree lower, but in fact
higher. He got a sixth order equation, but that was
not reducible to quadratic, like del Ferro's. He did not
conclude that the equation cannot be solved, however.

That conclusion is due to another Italian, Ruffini,
who realized that the quintic is so hard to solve because truly there is no closed form solution. Literally
in the last days of the 18th century he published a
book titled *General Theory of Equations*, in which he
proved his theorem. He based his proof on the connection of symmetry considerations and the concept
of permutations.

A transformation of an object, and let us focus on geometric objects, is a far reaching and very general concept. Another trichotomy greets us here as there are
three distinct transformations. They are translation,
rotation and reflection. A transformation is called a
symmetry if it preserves the object's structure and appearance. We review the concepts with the equilateral
triangle introduced earlier.

Rotating an equilateral triangle by 120 or 240 degrees obviously results in the same appearance, hence they are rotational symmetries. The rotation by zero degrees is also considered a symmetry, albeit a trivial one. Hence there are three rotational symmetries of the equilateral triangle. There are also three reflective symmetries, since the equilateral triangle is symmetric (in a mirror image sense) with respect to any bisector of its angles, as shown in Figure 10.1.

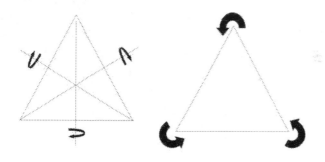

FIGURE 10.1 Symmetries of the equilateral triangle

Hence the equilateral triangle has six symmetries. Let us denote the vertices of an equilateral triangle by the letters X, Y, Z, in clockwise direction starting from the top. The six symmetries are described by the sequence of the letters corresponding to the changing locations of the vertices under the transformations as

$$X, Y, Z$$

$$Z, X, Y$$

$$Y, Z, X$$

$$X, Z, Y$$

$$Y, X, Z$$

and

$$Z, Y, X.$$

These are also the six possible permutations of three letters. In essence we obtained a bridge between the geometric transformations of the equilateral triangle and combinatoric computations where it is shown that the number of permutations of three objects is

$$3! = 1 \cdot 2 \cdot 3 = 6.$$

The ! notation is called a factorial whose generation rule is simply visible in the example.

Ruffini stated that permuting the solution of an equation should not make any difference in the outcome, i.e. the coefficients of the equation are symmetric with respect to algebraic operations on the roots. This is true for the six possible permutations of the cubic, it is even true for the 4! = 24 permutations of the quartic. Some algebraic equations, however, like the 5! = 120 permutations of the quintic do not admit such symmetric algebraic operations, hence those equations cannot be solved. His train of thought to prove the impossibility of the solution of the quintic was impeccable. However, due to a flaw in his proof his work was not accepted and his insight not acknowledged in his lifetime. He was, however, posthumously vindicated because the following correct proofs a generation later were based on his symmetry argument.

The credit for the proof finally went to two tragically short lived (not Italian) mathematicians; they both died in their twenties in the 1800s. The Norwegian Abel died of lung illness exacerbated by the harsh climate of his homeland. The French Galois died of his wound received in a duel related to his involvement in the unruly political climate of his homeland at the time. They proved, independently of each other but in very close temporal proximity, that no general closed formula solution to the quintic, or to any higher degree algebraic equation, exists.

Abel proved that an algebraic equation may be solvable by a formula (of admissible algebraic operations of addition, subtraction, multiplication and radicals) only if the set of permutations of the symmetries of the equation may be partitioned into specifically defined prime number subsets. While this is possible for the degree two, three and four equations, it cannot be done for any higher degree. He exploited the symmetry argument following the path Ruffini paved and his proof is sometimes called the Abel-Ruffini theorem.

Galois, starting from a different direction created a proof that became the foundation of a new branch of mathematics called group theory. He organized the possible number of permutations into groups and proved that only equations whose symmetry groups can be partitioned into specific, so-called normal subgroups may be solved. His proof was also reluctantly received by the mathematical elite because of its radically new approach and not fully accepted in his life.

Ultimately, the cubic turned out to be a barrier, albeit not impenetrable since the solution of the quartic existed (based on the cubic), but it was nevertheless a sentry guarding a territory of unsolvables. Now one could get rather philosophical about this topic. Why is our mathematics built such a way that there is only general solution up to degree four (that is solved by the help of three). Note, that this is a different question than the one Ruffini, Abel and Galois answered.

The question about why our mathematics is built that way remains unanswered, as many questions about the roles of three. Make no mistake about it, the discoveries of Ruffini and the others are just that, discoveries. They have not created the mathematical system that we are attempting to understand more deeply. We just have to keep wondering: who, how and why?

11

The tripod principle

The stability of a tripod is common knowledge, standing on three legs in many aspects of life is useful. Everyday applications are many, ranging from the photographers' mount to the three legged stool of the shoemaker. In an extension of this principle, many algebraic computations may be efficiently or exclusively executed by using three terms, three points or even three diagonals.

Three member sequences are sequences of numbers that are recursively defined based on three terms. One of the earliest such sequence was described by an amateur mathematician from Pisa, known by his nickname Fibonacci, in the early years of the 1200s. He described the sequence that is now forever associated with his name as a very simple, but very specific relation of three terms as

$$F_k = F_{k-1} + F_{k-2},$$

i.e. the next term in the sequence is always calculated from the prior two terms. This is the classical definition of a three member sequence.

The numbers to start his sequence are

$$F_0 = 0$$

and
$$F_1 = 1.$$

Then

$$F_2 = 0 + 1 = 1,$$

resulting in the sequence

$$F_k = 0, 1, 1, 2, 3, 5, 8, 13, \ldots.$$

Interestingly the ratio of two consecutive Fibonacci numbers asymptotically approaches the golden ratio, a topic of our geometric interest in an earlier chapter. When k is large

$$\frac{F_k}{F_{k-1}} \approx \frac{\sqrt{5} - 1}{2}.$$

Fibonacci in fact was interested in the solution of the third degree equation, a topic of the last chapter. He invented the sequence to find relations with irrational numbers of various radical expressions, such as the nested $\sqrt{a \pm \sqrt{b}}$ form. At his time these forms were hoped to lead to the elusive general solution of the cubic equation and we now know from the last chapter that he was on the right path.

Relying on three points is also adequate to produce good approximate solutions to various calculus problems. One such problem is to compute the derivative of a function. The derivative of a function geometrically is the slope of the tangent line to the function at a certain point. For certain classes of functions, this is easily executed by using the known derivative function. In practice, however, there are many cases where the derivative function is not simple and may not even be obtained in a closed form.

The three point finite difference method is based on three known points of the function, any one of which may be the location where the derivative is desired. Let the three given points be

$$(x_0, y_0), (x_1, y_1), (x_2, y_2),$$

and assume that they are sorted by their x coordinates in increasing order:

$$x_0 < x_1 < x_2.$$

In practical circumstances, where the three points may have been obtained by systematic measurements of some sort, the given points are quite often at equal distance from each other. For example using a distance h between the points results in

$$x_1 = x_0 + h,$$

and

$$x_2 = x_1 + h.$$

Let us first seek the derivative of the function at the middle point. The following extremely simple formula gives the approximate derivative of the function at the middle point

$$f'(x_1) = \frac{f(x_0) - f(x_2)}{2h}.$$

This is of course geometrically nothing else but the slope of the chord between the two extreme points. Clearly, the distance of the points influences the quality of the approximation, nevertheless, three points is

all we needed. Given the same three points, one can
also compute the derivative at either end point. For
example calculating the derivative at the left end point
may be done by

$$f'(x_0) = \frac{-3f(x_0) + 4f(x_1) - f(x_2)}{2h}.$$

Here the calculation was based on by looking ahead
and using the next two points in front of the target
x_0 point, hence the formula is known as the forward
looking three point formula. The coefficients are established in order to account for that imbalance. A backward difference three point formula is easily obtained
by simply reversing the order of the three points.

Another fundamental problem of calculus, integra-
tion of a function in an interval may also be very efficiently and accurately solved by the three point approach. The problem's geometric meaning is the area
between a certain curve and a segment of the x axis
defined by the boundary points as

$$a = x_0$$

and

$$b = x_2.$$

The intermediate point will be chosen at the middle
as above in the differentiation case. The very efficient
and still widely used formula first described by the
British mathematician Simpson in the 18th century is

$$\int_a^b f(x)dx = \frac{h}{3}(f(x_0) + 4f(x_1) + f(x_2)).$$

The geometric insight here is that each segment of the
function is in essence replaced by a parabola. The

method may be extended to a set of many points that is traversed by a strategy involving three points at a time. For example for five points

$$a = x_0 < x_1 < x_2 < x_3 < x_4 = b$$

the formula is

$$\int_a^b f(x)dx =$$

$$\frac{h}{3}(f(x_0) + 4f(x_1) + 2f(x_2) + 4f(x_3) + f(x_4)).$$

The pattern is clearly visible, the boundary function values have a unit multiplier, the odd numbered values are multiplied by 4 and the even numbered terms by 2. This can be extended to any number of points. In practical cases the process is actually of the reverse. Starting from a sample of three points a gradual refinement may be executed by introducing intermediate points as necessary to improve the accuracy of the solution. The number of refinement points depends on the smoothness of the function, or lack thereof.

The significant contribution of the number three is in the ability to capture the local tendencies of the function in the vicinity of the point of interest. The concept of traversing a larger set by steps of three may be carried even further, resulting in the three member recurrences.

Three member recurrences are similar to the three member sequences, like that of Fibonacci, but defined in terms of functions. A well known and very practical three member recurrence is due to Chebyshev, a Russian mathematician who published it in the early

1800s. The Chebyshev recurrence is defined by the relation of three terms as

$$T_{k+1}(x) = 2xT_k(x) - T_{k-1}(x).$$

Starting with $T_0(x) = 1$ and $T_1(x) = x$ the recurrence proceeds with $T_2(x) = 2x^2 - 1$ and $T_3(x) = 4x^3 - 3x$. These Chebishev polynomials exhibit interesting symmetry characteristics that significantly contribute to their usefulness in approximating functions.

One can compute coefficients a_k to obtain an approximation to a function as

$$f(x) \approx a_0T_0(x) + a_1T_1(x) + a_2T_2(x) + \ldots$$

This form is significant in approximating periodic functions as it provides a practical and sometimes more efficient alternative to Fourier approximation. The Chebyshev approximation is important in many practical circumstances approximating nontrivial periodic functions.

The usefulness of the three member recurrences is widespread and it does not end in approximations. There are other three member recurrences that have a role in reducing matrices to tridiagonal forms. Tridiagonal forms are another extremely important occurrence of the three, manifesting another gateway to infinity

A matrix A is an arrangement of numerical terms in rows and columns as

$$A = \begin{bmatrix} a_{11} \ a_{12} \ a_{13} \ \ldots \\ a_{21} \ a_{22} \ a_{23} \ \ldots \\ a_{31} \ a_{32} \ a_{33} \ \ldots \\ \ldots \ldots \ldots \ldots \end{bmatrix}.$$

Here the dots indicate that the matrix could be of any number of rows and columns. For every square matrix, whose number of rows and columns are the same, a very important problem called the eigenvalue problem is defined as

$$A\varphi = \lambda\varphi,$$

where the λ scalar multiplier is an eigenvalue and the φ vector is an eigenvector of the matrix. For a matrix of order three, there are three eigenvalues and eigenvectors. They have also been called principal value and vector in the past, but the German originated term eigenvalue, meaning the matrix's own value, stuck. Admittedly we are at the limits of our allotted mathematical depth therefore the following is kept relatively simple and conversational.

The physical meaning of the eigenvalue and eigenvector is extremely important when the matrix describes some practical phenomenon. For example, when the matrix describes the dynamic behavior of a structure, like a bridge or an airplane wing, the eigenvalue is the so-called resonance frequency at which the structure becomes unstable. The corresponding eigenvector depicts the shape of the structure at the unstable scenario.

The geometrical meaning of the eigenvalues and eigenvectors is related to an ellipsoid represented by the

matrix. This ellipsoid, imagine a football as shown in
Figure 11.1, is rotated with respect to the coordinate
axes denoted by x_1, x_2 and x_3 in the figure.

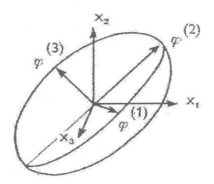

FIGURE 11.1 Principal axes of ellipsoid

The geometrical meaning of the three eigenvectors,
denoted by $(\varphi^{(1)}, \varphi^{(2)}, \varphi^{(3)})$ in the figure, is to specify
the direction of the so-called principal axes of the el-
lipsoid and the eigenvalues are proportional with the
length of the principal axes. These correspond to the
the longest and shortest dimensions of the football.
Note that there are two identical shortest directions
of the football, as it is symmetric with respect to its
longitudinal axis. This is not necessarily true for a
general matrix. Otherwise, the analogy holds, at least
in three dimensions. In higher order matrices we need
to imagine a higher dimensional football, somewhat of

a mental challenge, so we leave it at that.

Unfortunately, directly computing the eigenvalues
and eigenvectors is expensive, especially when the size
of the matrix is large. The computational cost is proportional to the third power of the number of rows of
the matrix. To execute this in a practical case of a
million rows is impossible even with the most modern
computers.

Luckily, there is a three member recurrence invented
by the Hungarian mathematician Cornelius Lanczos in
the middle of the last century that is uniquely suited
to execute the transformation of the matrix to a tridiagonal form, a matrix having non-zero terms only in
three diagonals. Such tridiagonal form is

$$T = \begin{bmatrix} t_{11} & t_{12} & 0 & 0 \\ t_{21} & t_{22} & t_{23} & 0 \\ 0 & t_{32} & t_{33} & \ldots \\ 0 & 0 & \ldots & \ldots \end{bmatrix}.$$

Here the dots represent nonzero values in the contin-
uation of the matrix. The three member Lanczos recurrence calculates three terms of a certain row of the
tridiagonal matrix in each step of the recurrence. The
prevalence of three is overbearing, but it does not end
there. The importance of this tridiagonal form is also
threefold.

First of all, this form retains the original λ eigenvalues of the matrix as implied by the equation

$$T\overline{\varphi} = \lambda\overline{\varphi}.$$

The $\bar{\varphi}$ eigenvectors of the tridiagonal form are somewhat different, as indicated by the bar, but the original
φ eigenvectors of the matrix are easily recovered from
them.

Secondly, the eigenvalues of the tridiagonal form may
be found with significantly less computational cost.
This may not be highly visible from the example matrices above, but the higher the matrix size the larger
the number of zero terms in the tridiagonal form and
that produces tremendous computational advantages.

Thirdly, there is no method that executes a more
condensed reduction with finite number of operations.
There is a method originally developed by the Prus-
sian mathematician Jacobi in the first half of the 1800s
that aspired to find a single diagonal form. The problem is that the number of operational steps to reach
the form might be infinite.

It appears that the tridiagonal form of a matrix is
optimal in the sense that it is the most compact form
retaining the eigenvalues of the matrix that is still at-
tainable by small, finite number of operations, another
gateway to the infinity, indeed.

12

Ternary sets and counting infinity

We ease into the ultimate connection between three and infinity by considering so-called ternary sets. Such sets are defined by the process of repeatedly removing a third of a set while applying some rule recursively. A special ternary set defined by Cantor in the late 1880s is obtained by recursively removing the middle third of a certain line segment.

For example, considering the interval $[0, 1]$ of the number-line, the first step would remove the points inside of the interval $[\frac{1}{3}, \frac{2}{3}]$. Note that the boundaries of the removed segment are not removed, resulting in the set of two segments $[0, \frac{1}{3}]$ and $[\frac{2}{3}, 1]$. The second recurrence results in the removal of the middle thirds of both segments $[\frac{1}{9}, \frac{2}{9}]$ and $[\frac{7}{9}, \frac{8}{9}]$. The remaining set consists of four segments now, they are

$$[0, \frac{1}{9}],$$

$$[\frac{2}{9}, \frac{3}{9}] = [\frac{2}{9}, \frac{1}{3}],$$

$$[\frac{6}{9}, \frac{7}{9}] = [\frac{2}{3}, \frac{7}{9}]$$

and

$$[\frac{8}{9}, 1].$$

Note the missing middle third removed first, and the missing ninths removed now. If we continued the process we would remove a $\frac{1}{27}$ long middle segment from each of the four segments resulting in the remaining set of

$$[0, \frac{1}{27}], \; [\frac{2}{27}, \frac{3}{27}],$$

$$[\frac{6}{27}, \frac{7}{27}], \; [\frac{8}{27}, \frac{9}{27}],$$

$$[\frac{18}{27}, \frac{19}{27}], \; [\frac{20}{27}, \frac{21}{27}],$$

and

$$[\frac{24}{27}, \frac{25}{27}], \; [\frac{26}{27}, 1].$$

The next step would be the removal of eight $\frac{1}{81}$ long segments and so on. The total length of the segments removed is

$$\frac{1}{3} + \frac{2}{9} + \frac{4}{27} + \frac{8}{81} + \ldots$$

This is of course a simple geometric series with a starting term of $\frac{1}{3}$ and a quotient of $\frac{2}{3}$, for which the sum is the known expression of

$$\frac{1}{3} \frac{1}{1 - \frac{2}{3}} = 1.$$

It appears that if we continued the process indefinitely, we would remove the complete segment we started with. This, however, contradicts the fact that the boundaries of each segment remained in the set. A seriously counterintuitive result, indeed.

It is even more intriguing that there are many points remaining in the set that are not interval end-points, they are interior to a segment. For example, let us consider the decimal number $\frac{3}{10}$. Since

$$\frac{2}{9} = \frac{20}{90} < \frac{27}{90} = \frac{3}{10}$$

and

$$\frac{3}{10} = \frac{27}{90} < \frac{30}{90} = \frac{3}{9}$$

or

$$\frac{2}{9} < \frac{3}{10} < \frac{3}{9},$$

it remained in the set after the second removal. In the third removal it will also remain because

$$\frac{8}{27} = \frac{80}{270} < \frac{81}{270} = \frac{3}{10}$$

and

$$\frac{3}{10} = \frac{81}{270} < \frac{90}{270} = \frac{9}{27},$$

or

$$\frac{8}{27} < \frac{3}{10} < \frac{9}{27}.$$

It will remain in the set forever, no matter how many more steps we execute. It is rather mind-boggling how the simple concept of removing a third of a simple unit long segment results in such conundrum. The reason of this of course lies in the fact that the original set, the points of the unit long segment, was infinite. In the case of infinite sets all common sense appears to be lost.

The paradoxical nature of infinity dates back to the early Greek thinkers, most notably to Xeno of the 5th

century BC whose famous mind experiment involving
Achilles and the tortoise has stunned people for many
centuries and sometimes even today. In this exercise
Xeno claimed that in a race between Achilles and a
tortoise, if the tortoise is allowed a certain distance
head start, say ten meters on a hundred meter course,
Achilles will never be able catch up with it.

His argument was that by the time Achilles reached
the point where the tortoise started from, the tortoise
had moved ahead. Achilles will reach the tortoise's
new position again just to find that the tortoise has already left. And so on. The dilemma of course is rooted
in the question whether a finite amount of anything
can be subdivided into pieces of smaller and smaller
size ad infinitum, or after a while one reaches a finite
small piece that cannot be divided further.

The argument was also applied to the universe as
a whole. On one side was the finite universe model
which went hand in hand with the Earth centric philosophy of the Catholic church. On the other side was
the infinite universe belief that cost Giordano Bruno
his life at the stake in 1600.

That event made other scientists harboring infinite
universal views very careful. The famous Galileo himself, about three decades after Bruno's death, was trying to compromise by acknowledging that our finite
mind is unable to comprehend infinity of numbers (hid-
ing the fact that he believed in the infinity of numbers).
Even this clever parsing did not save him from house
arrest of many years and only his personal connection
to the Pope saved him from sharing Giordano Bruno's

fate.

Still, in about 50 years the war was over. The church
had no control over the German Leibniz's work on the
infinitesimal, and the English Newton's infinitely small
increments leading to what we call today calculus. The
church gave up teaching and defending the concept of
indivisibility by the 1650s. Soon after that the also
English Wallis in 1655 introduced the symbol ∞ that
we still use today. He explained it as a curve that has
no beginning or end and could be traveled through infinite number of times. By specifying a special symbol
for it, however, he opened up Pandora's box. Having a
symbol for infinity implied that it is a certain number.
Then how big is it? And another war started about
counting the infinity.

The numerability of infinite sets became a subject of
enormous interest and cause of arguments about the
impossibility of finding the actual value of the infinite.
Some considered it a philosophical possibility, but not
a countable practicality. Cantor, however, realized
that one can count infinite sets by rendering a one
to one correspondence between the set and the counting numbers. Such a set he called denumerable and
turned the mathematics of the infinite upside down,
nothing short of a revolution.

Counting sets of the infinite was Cantor's everlast-
ing contribution to number theory. Set theory itself
was significantly shaped by Cantor's contemporary,
the German Dedekind. He proposed the separation
of the rational number line into two sets by any irrational number, nowadays called a Dedekind cut. He

was also a big supporter of Cantor's ideas that were at
the time not universally embraced by the mathematical community.

Some of Cantor's contemporaries did not agree with
his approach. In fact his one time mathematics profes-
sor, Kronecker of the δ fame had vehemently opposed
Cantor's work going as far as blocking some of Cantor's publications. It is now assumed that it was plain
professional jealousy of a teacher who was not rejoiced
by the accomplishment of his student, a sad sentiment.

Or maybe he just did not understand it. Our in-
tuition, after all, tells us that there are many more
rational numbers than integers. There are several rational numbers between each pair of two consecutive
integers, so this seems very plausible. Cantor, however, ingeniously arranged the infinite number of rational numbers into the two dimensional array

$$\frac{1}{1} \quad \frac{2}{1} \quad \frac{3}{1} \quad \frac{4}{1} \quad \cdots$$
$$\frac{1}{2} \quad \frac{2}{2} \quad \frac{3}{2} \quad \frac{4}{2} \quad \cdots$$
$$\frac{1}{3} \quad \frac{2}{3} \quad \frac{3}{3} \quad \frac{4}{3} \quad \cdots$$
$$\frac{1}{4} \quad \frac{2}{4} \quad \frac{3}{4} \quad \frac{4}{4} \quad \cdots$$
$$\cdots \quad \cdots \quad \cdots \quad \cdots \quad \cdots$$

The first column of the arrangement contains all natural fractions less than one, while the first row contains
all integers. He then proposed traversing this array by
stepping one to the right, then diagonally down, one
step down and diagonally up recursively, until all the

fractions are covered. Since there are fractions that occur repeatedly, for example all the diagonal terms of the array are one, he proposed ignoring those. Following this process, he laid out all rational numbers in a row and created the one to one correspondence with the natural numbers as

$$\frac{1}{1}, \quad \frac{2}{1}, \quad \frac{1}{2}, \quad \frac{1}{3}, \quad \frac{3}{1}, \quad \frac{4}{1}, \quad \frac{3}{2}, \quad \frac{2}{3}, \ldots,$$

$$1, \quad 2, \quad 3, \quad 4, \quad 5, \quad 6, \quad 7, \quad 8, \ldots,$$

where the repeated numbers were ignored. This process enabled "counting" all rational numbers, the rational number set was denumerable. He introduced a number $\mathcal{N}_0$ as the size of any set that may be denumerable by the natural numbers. This was called the cardinality of the natural number set. This by far did not mean that all infinite sets were of the same order.

The next in Cantor's quest was the set of algebraic numbers, numbers that may be obtained as the root of the polynomial equations with integer coefficients. The rational numbers constitute a subset of this set. In 1874 Cantor showed that the set of algebraic numbers is also countable, and its cardinality is also $\mathcal{N}_0$.

Then the transcendental numbers captured Cantor's attention. Transcendental numbers, as we defined them in an earlier chapter are numbers that cannot be obtained as the root of polynomial equations with integer coefficients, and as such comprise the complementary set of the algebraic numbers. The famous transcendental number pointed out before, the π is an example of such. While this would imply that such numbers are rare, that is far from the truth. In fact there are many more transcendental numbers (albeit few such notable as the π) than rational numbers. Cantor ultimately demonstrated that the set of transcendental numbers is uncountable after showing that the real numbers are uncountable as follows.

He proposed to find a one to one correspondence between the points on a line and the natural numbers. Let us simplify the problem by restricting the length of the line to be one. Any point on the unit segment is described by its distance from the start of the segment, so it is a decimal number of infinite decimal digits. Let us assume that we can write all such numbers in a list of form

$$0.a_1 a_2 a_3 \ldots$$

$$0.b_1 b_2 b_3 \ldots$$

$$0.c_1 c_2 c_3 \ldots$$

$$0.d_1 d_2 d_3 \ldots$$

$$\ldots$$

We could match this list with the natural numbers and count it as order $\mathcal{N}_0$. Cantor himself, however, gave a counterexample. He created a new number in addition to all the numbers on the line segment with the following logic. He used for the first digit any other number than a_1, for the second digit any other number but b_2, and so on until infinity. The new number is obviously not on the list, however, we assumed that the list was complete, hence a contradiction arose.

The assumption that all the real numbers of a line segment can be arranged and counted by the natural number set was false. Hence this set is uncountable, the order of this infinity is higher than that of the order of the natural numbers. This second order of infinity is called $\mathcal{N}_1$, the cardinality of the real numbers. This is obviously applicable to a line segment of any length, not just the unit long as shown in the following.

We can make a one to one correspondence between any two line segments. Imagine a simple right triangle an draw a vertical line from every point on the horizontal side to the hypotenuse. Clearly for every point on the horizontal side we can find a corresponding point on the hypotenuse. The hypotenuse, however, is obviously longer than the sides, hence it must have some extra points left, mustn't?

Well, not. Imagine that the process was started from the hypotenuse and drew a line from every point of the hypotenuse to the horizontal line. The one to one correspondence may be established just as well. Clearly any line segment can be placed in a one to one correspondence with any other. Hence the order of the set of points on any finite line segment is $\mathcal{N}_1$.

So far the focus was on a finite subset of the continuum, that is the real numbers. Cantor, however, was striving to find a measure of the continuum in general, for example a line of infinite length, such as the number line. He assumed that the measure of the continuum is the same as $\mathcal{N}_1$ and spent the rest of his life trying to prove it to no avail. This statement is still known as Cantor's continuum hypothesis.

Other schools of thought proposed a generalized continuum hypothesis stating that the cardinality of the continuum is a different value yet again: $\mathcal{N}_2$. The continuum hypothesis was proven to be unprovable with some very intricate arguments by the American mathematician Cohen in the 1960s. He based his arguments on the German Gödel's incompleteness theorem form the 1940s.

Whether one assumes Cantor's assertion of $\mathcal{N}_1$ or an even larger $\mathcal{N}_2$, the process, however, appears to end at this point. According to our present understanding these three infinite orders enable us to count anything and everything in our universe.

We cannot fathom why there would be three of these fundamental infinite orders, but it is certainly another intriguing presence of three.

13

From trifoliates to triple points

In this chapter we focus on the occurrences of the number three in our biological and physical lives. There are many biological occurrences of the number three. The number of flowers and trees having three petals or leaves, commonly called trifoliates, is astonishingly large. Just think of the clover-leaf (apart from the accidental proverbial fourth leaf) shown on the left hand side of Figure 13.1.

FIGURE 13.1 Trifoliate and trifolium

Now if you think of this being an accident of nature with no connection with mathematics whatsoever, think twice. There are very appealing mathematical functions, called trifoliums that are generated with ease from simple implicit expressions. Well, the simplicity of the expression may be an exaggeration, but the beauty of the shape and its agreement with nature is surely demonstrated on the right hand side of Figure 13.1

Furthermore, nature consists of three different classes of things, mineral, vegetal and animal. It is also very interesting that there are three common symmetry arrangements of living organisms, spherical, radial and bilateral. Bilateral symmetry is manifested in the intriguing patterns of butterflies, symmetric with respect to a plane cutting through the body. We humans by and large belong to the class of bilaterally symmetric organisms, so do most of the animals. Radial symmetry is with respect to an axis going through the center of the body. Examples of such are various sea creatures like jellyfish. Finally, spherical symmetry is a characteristic of a body that is symmetric with respect to a center point. Sphere like organisms, like cells exhibit this symmetry.

A most intriguing biological fact is related to the optical white light of physics, that is a composite of several colors. Three of these component colors are red, green and blue. The biological consequence of these three colors is the human vision property called trichromacy manifested by the visual receptors of our eyes absorbing at three different wavelengths. Figure 13.2 shows the absorption of the three receptors in our eyes.

The longer range receptors (L) are most sensitive to the wavelength around 580 nanometers. That unit

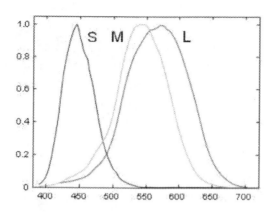

FIGURE 13.2 Human vision absorption

is 10^{-9} meter, or a thousandth of a thousandth of a millimeter, a very small unit indeed. The middle range (M) receptors are best in the range of 535 to 545 nanometers and the shortest range (S) receptors operate somewhat apart with a peak sensitivity at 440 nanometers. These three receptors sense the red, green and blue lights, respectively.

The other colors of life are created in the mind's palette of mixing. We perceive yellow when both the long range (red) and the medium range (green) receptors are stimulated at the same time to a certain extent. Other mixed colors appear where the sensitivity profiles of the receptors overlap.

This wonderful pairing of our vision with the optics enables us to perceive the full spectrum by mixing three fundamental colors. This capacity is intriguingly only shared by humans and some primates: it does not permeate the animal kingdom. Hence, it clearly indicates an evolutionary origin; it was developed after the humans and primates branched off of the main tree of life. The occurrence of three components here may only be the outcome of nature's adherence to the reality, that of biology to the physical optics, but intriguing nevertheless.

The number three is prominently present in many other facets of physics, ranging from mechanics to fluids. Classical mechanics contains a large number of trichotomies. There are many natural laws describing phenomena among three fundamental quantities: Newton's second law is a great example. It is the well known formula of force = mass · acceleration, or

$$F = m \cdot a.$$

This is an instrumental law of our everyday physics, the dynamics of moving bodies, let them be human, or automobiles or even airplanes. The law may be written in the triangular (!) arrangement of

$$\frac{F}{m \cdot a}$$

enabling the easy calculation of any of the three terms by covering it up and looking at the remainder. For example, covering up mass results in

$$\frac{F}{a}$$

which means we need to divide the force by the acceleration to obtain the mass of an object. Similarly one can compute the acceleration by covering it up.

Covering up the force results of course in the original law.

The most relevant manifestation of this law in our lives is our weight, which is

$$G = m \cdot g,$$

where g is the acceleration of gravity. This law is the reason why the same person weighs less on the Moon than here on Earth. The acceleration of gravity on the smaller mass of Moon is smaller, our mass does not change by traveling there.

Interestingly this is only one of three (again) of Newton's laws of motion, in fact it is the second. The first law states that a body under a constant motion will remain in such until an external force is applied to it. The third states the also well known "for every action there is a reaction", originally meant for physical forces, but a phrase in household use nowadays.

Considering the mass of the above law, it is also the outcome of another triad of mass = density · volume, or

$$m = \rho \cdot V.$$

Clearly a low density material (such as for example a gas) in a large volume could provide a certain amount of mass. Conversely, a large density material (such as for example a metal) could produce the same amount of mass in a much lesser volume. The triangular arrangement of

$$\frac{m}{\rho \cdot V}$$

applies for this triad as well. Finally the third triad
related to Newton's law is that of the acceleration. A
velocity v reached by accelerating a body for a time
duration of t is

$$v = a \cdot t,$$

or with the now familiar

$$\frac{v}{a \cdot t}$$

computational triangle. The time required to reach
the velocity is obtained by covering up t, resulting in
v/a, and the rest of the relations follow.

In summary, the second of the three laws of Newton
led to a triangular relation between the three quantities participating and in turn each of those three
quantities are comprised of a triad. Our Newtonian
mechanical world is built of a wonderful tree of threes.

Stepping out of our Newtonian mechanical world
into our Solar system produces other interesting trichotomies. The fact that we occupy the third planet
from the Sun was not lost on us humans, ever since
we were able to see the planets. Some people consider
this fact to be the reason for the prominence of the
number three in our everyday life. But, after reading
about the mathematical roles in the prior chapters, we
know it must be more.

The planetary motions are also described by three
rules, mathematically first stated by the Austrian high
school teacher turned astronomer Kepler in the early
years of 1600s. He became an assistant to the Danish

astronomer Tycho Brahe whose meticulous observations during the second half of the 1500s provided the basis for Kepler's laws. They are:

1. The orbit of a planet is an ellipse with the Sun in one of the focal points.

2. The sector covered by the line between the planet and the Sun is equal in equal time intervals.

3. The time of a planet's orbit around the Sun is directly proportional to the third (!) power of the square root of the semi-major axis of the ellipse of the orbit.

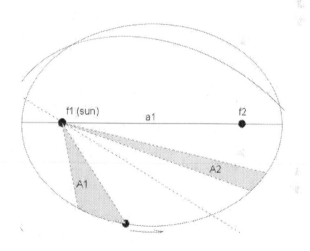

FIGURE 13.3 Kepler's laws of planetary motion

Figure 13.3 demonstrates the laws with a planet orbiting the Sun located in one of the focal points (f_1) of an elliptical orbit as stated by the first law. When the planet is at the closest to the focus point containing the Sun, it is at perihelion. The opposite of that is the aphelion. The sectors A_1 and A_2 depicted on the figure are of the same area according to the second law. Finally, the orbit time of the planet is proportional to third power of the square root of the half of the distance a_1.

Another planet, with a different axis of orbit but with a common focal point (slant dotted line in the figure going through f_1) could have an orbit crossing that of the first one as shown in the figure with the partial ellipse. This is not an uncommon occurrence in some planetary systems, but in most cases the planes of the ellipses are not the same, so there is no chance for a catastrophic collision.

On a side note, Kepler may be considered the original proponent of the intelligent design movement of nowadays. He was convinced that God has created the universe according to an intelligent plan that would be accessible to us mere humans through studying and reasoning.

There are further physical disciplines where Newton-like three member laws apply. For example in electric circuits the relationship between the voltage (U), the current (I) and resistance (R) is called Ohm's law:

$$U = I \cdot R.$$

Other analogies exist in other physical principles, for example in fluid mechanics. The mention of fluids brings forth one of the most intrinsic presences of three in our lives.

Most inorganic materials surrounding us in our lives occur in three phases, fluid, solid and gaseous. The fact of having three is surprising sometimes because we are used to one particular phase of certain materials. Metals used by us are mostly solid and we do not think about them being liquid, albeit they certainly are during their manufacturing process involving melting. Even more pronounced is our bias when it gets to gases. Oxygen, the gas sustaining our lives, is seldom thought as being a liquid although it is in that form when it propels the space shuttle into orbit.

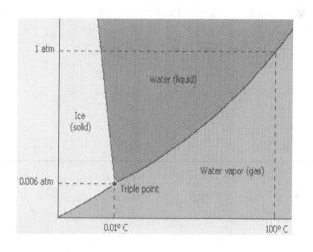

FIGURE 13.4 Triple point of water

The phases of materials occur in special temperature and pressure domains as shown in Figure 13.4 with the pressure as vertical axis and temperature as horizontal axis. The figure shows the phases of the fundamental fluid of our lives, the water, with its solid form of ice and its gas form of water vapor.

Water also exhibits a special triple point where all three phases coexist. It is a delicately balanced unique point at 0.01 Celsius temperature and at approximately 0.006 atmospheric pressure, not necessarily everyday circumstances. It is very far from the normal conditions of our lives at 1 atmosphere and somewhere below 100 Celsius, comfortably around 20. Around the triple point water can change phases while bypassing intermediate stages.

For example, below the triple point pressure water can go from solid state to gaseous state, i.e. heating ice could result in water vapor (steam) without melting. This process is called sublimation, while its opposite, going from vapor to solid, is called deposition. In the case of water, the latter one is the well known phenomenon of frost formation.

The presence of three in this physics domain is as beguiling as elsewhere. It is after all conceivable that there are other worlds were some creatures emerged adapting themselves to different physics. Just imagine a world where atmospheric pressure is very low and the habitants live in the region well below the triple point. They will never encounter the fluid phase of water, they live in an ice and vapor world.

14

Everyday trichotomies

Comprehending all the fundamental roles of the number three in our physical lives may be beyond our grasp, but those many roles might just be the reason why three has reached such a prominence in our everyday life. There are many occurrences of the number three in our everyday life ranging from superstition and literature, through sports and folklore, to education and government. There are a mind-boggling number of trichotomies in our life.

Let's look at the superstitious uses of the number three. Sometimes, it is a lucky occurrence as in "third time is a charm". Sometimes it reflects a melancholic sentiment like the expression "three times a bridesmaid, never a bride". Thirdly, it is sometimes gloomy as in "going down for the third time". In many occasions the "morning, noon, and night" time trichotomy is used in correspondence with the three ages of man, young, middle aged and old.

Literary references also abound; think of the Three muskateers of Dumas and the Three sisters of Chekhov. There are also the three monkeys in the literature of several Asian cultures, the ones who do not hear, see or say evil.

Sport, especially our national game baseball, is full of trichotomies. There are three bases, three strikes, three outs just to get started. There are three out-fielders and one of the most coveted hits, apart from a home run, is a triple. We keep track of a team's performance in three measures of runs, hits and errors. Batting and fielding percentages are calculated to three decimals and the earned run average of pitchers is kept for three digits.

In many international sport events, Olympics and world cups of various sports, there are three medals, gold, silver and bronze. There are three winning scenarios in horse racing: win, place and show; and who can forget the most coveted price of horse racing: the Triple Crown. The outcomes of a game between two teams in most sports are win, loose or draw. A player scoring three times in a game achieves a hat trick.

Then there are the best of three sets and games in various sports ranging from ping-pong to volleyball. Iron-men competitions consists of three sports, swimming, biking and running. There are three (plus one) downs in American football and even in cricket there is a triple in having three wickets on each side of the pitch. Finally, three ropes in a boxing ring and the famous three ring circus close this impressive, but undoubtedly incomplete list.

We have a tendency to use three lettered acronyms in our life, ranging from government organizations, such as IRS and FBI, through associations like MAA (Mathematical Association of America) and the AMA (American Medical Association), all the way to famous persons like FDR and JFK. Then we use three letter acronyms for unions (SAG for Screen Actors Guild) and television stations (ABC, NBC, CBS, PBS and even FOX, although that is a stretch). We also learn the ABC-s in the elementary school, we do not learn the ABCDE-s.

Moving on to folklore we find many wonderfully expressive triples. Think of "hook, line and sinker", "fat, dumb and happy", "blood, sweat and tears", "signed sealed and delivered", "lock, stock and barrel". The list goes on: we all have "things to do, places to go and people to see". Then we say "in any way, shape or form", "going, going and gone", "ready, set, go" and "give me three reasons why...". The list is surprisingly long and thought provoking.

When we tell jokes, there are many with three participants. Commonly told jokes use the Englishman, the Irishman and the Scot; or the minister, the priest and the rabbi. And let us not forget the jokes about the blond, the brunette and the redhead; or the ones about the lawyer, the engineer and the doctor.

We eat three meals a day, have three course meals mainly and three plates. Usually we use three utensils to eat our meals: a spoon, a fork and a knife. One of the most popular sandwiches, the club sandwich, is a triple decker. Another favorite, the BLT sandwich mixes our penchant for the three letter acronyms with three components in bacon, lettuce and tomato. We could have our steaks rare, medium and well done; and finish our meal with coffee, tea or an after dinner drink. Triples and triples galore in the kitchen.

We play games like Tic-Tac-Doe (three words with
three characters each) in which the winning is accomplished by getting three symbols of the player in a row
or column. We also play card games with three face
cards (Jack, Queen and King) that some interpret as
a manifestation of the son, mother and father.

When we get outside of our homes, we are confronted
by triples everywhere. Our car is in neutral when we
start and we can move out of the garage by either in
reverse or in forward and we will find three colors on
the traffic lights at the street corners: red, yellow and
green. We may drive on a three lane highway, and if
it is on a freeway, we have the next three exists posted
usually. We could use nickels, dimes and quarters at
the public telephones before the onset of cell-phones.

Our education system consists of three major levels, primary (elementary), secondary (high school) and
higher (colleges and universities). In the elementary
schools the proverbial three R's are being taught; they
are "Reading, wRiting and aRithmetic". The higher
institutions grant three degrees in their respective fields,
Bachelor's, Master's and Doctoral. The distinguished
degrees also come in three grades: cum laude, magna
cum laude and summa cum laude. The instructors
at higher institutions have three grades: assistant, associate and full professors. There is even a tongue
in cheek trichotomy in the saying "those who can, do;
those who can't teach; and those who can't teach teach
the teachers".

Then we speak in three, past, present and future

tenses. We have three pronouns in first, second and third person. The third person has three versions in he, she or it, as genders are masculine, feminine and neutral. There are three major sentence types, declarative, exclamatory and interrogative, punctuated in writing with period, explanation mark and question mark. There are the three versions of adjectives like good, better and best, or bad, worse and worst.

Possibly inherited from the Roman triumvirates, already mentioned in the very first chapter, our democratic political system has three branches, the executive, legislative and the judicial branches. The branches represent a certain symmetry of balancing power. One person could easily succumb to the temptations of power and become a tyrant. Two members in power could create a stalemate, an unresolvable conflict that may be resolved by the removal of one, hence the system becoming a potential tyranny. Three members, however, may always strike a balance by majority and ensure the benefit of the masses. A system of great insight from two thousand years ago, but of practical importance today.

Another trichotomy, life, liberty and pursuit of happiness, is in our Constitution and our government is "of the people, by the people and for the people" although some might argue with that.

Our military forces are also of three major branches: Army, Navy and Air Force (categorizing the heroic Marines into the Navy). The officer class in all branches is comprised of three ranks and three grades in each rank. Looking at the Navy, there are ensigns, junior lieutenants and lieutenants in the junior officer rank. There are lieutenant commanders, commanders and captains in the senior official rank. Finally, there are rear, vice and full admirals in the flag officer rank of the Navy.

These trichotomies are admittedly not based on an inherent tripartite functionality; they are mainly artifacts of our special inclination toward the number three. They may also be employed because of the symmetry and balance, or tie breaking forte provided by the number three. Nevertheless, they prove that after occupying a prominent role in the human history for thousands of years and demonstrating an intrinsic presence in our physical life, the number three has now fully permeated our everyday life.

15

Three of life

It is by now quite clear that three was a fundamental number in the beginning of counting by humankind, sort of the gateway to multiplicity. In many ancient number schemes it shared a symbol with one and two. After three came the use of some new symbols or arrangements. This aspect can, however, be considered only as a human convenience in the learning process.

The importance of triangles as a fundamental building block of geometry is undeniable. The misleading simplicity of the object hides very powerful capabilities. The mechanical advantages of triangular structures spread into all kinds of engineering fields. The frames of many bridges are constructed of triangular truss components. Even rectangular frames of high rises require corner triangles to prevent the folding of the structure. A triangular structure cannot ever fold. There is no other structural component that could replace it. This is such a powerful capability that it will keep the triangle an intrinsic component of our **lives** forever.

Then we come to trigonometry bridging geometry and algebra. The computations involving trigonometry are far away from actual geometric problems. One can say that the trigonometric functions are as fundamental building blocks of algebra as the actual triangles are of geometry. Periodic functions describe many processes in physical **life** and they are either comprised of or well approximated by trigonometric components.

Our physical universe, at least on our scale, is of three dimensions. Most physical phenomena are described in three dimensional coordinate systems and the mathematics involved is simple. Simplicity of mathematics almost always implies the optimal, and likely correct, interpretation of a phenomenon. Time as the fourth dimension on a relativistic scale or hypothetical string dimensions aside, we **live** in three dimensions.

The power of three in polynomials lead to the powerful computational tools of cubic splines. They have ancient and modern engineering as well as human applications. In human applications they are able to describe the most important physical objects in our **lives**, our bodies.

We have also established the fact that doing various activities in three steps or describing certain things in three components is very advantageous. The tridiagonal form of matrices is nothing short of spectacular. Retaining the complete spectral characteristics of a matrix with only three diagonals and the ensuing necessity of potentially infinite number of operations to go further is intriguing. This leads to the murky territory of the three as a gateway to or gate-keeper of infinity, the least understood part of our **life** in philosophical, physical or mathematical sense.

Epilogue

Starting from archaeological and historical appearances of the number three we arrived at its use in our physical world and everyday life, justifying the ambitious title. We have also completed a journey through its considerable mathematical domain.

There are many more significant mathematical occurrences of the number three in describing mechanical phenomena of our lives by natural laws that can be cast into a form involving three in various ways. Those fell outside our focus restricted by the level of mathematics we aimed to explore.

It would be rather presumptuous to assume that we understand the reasons for the unique roles of the number three. It can only be hoped that this journey illuminated its mystic and magic, its practical importance or impossible barrier nature, capturing the reader's imagination and instigating further thoughts.

While a unifying connection between the occurrences of three is elusive, hopefully it will become clearer in the future enhancing our rudimentary understanding of the universe. After all, time also exhibits three distinct stages: past, present and future.

Literature

[1] R. J. Atkinson; Stonehenge, Penguin Books, 1956

[2] John Derbyshire; Prime obsession: Bernhard Riemann and the greatest unsolved problem in mathematics, Plume, New York, 2004

[3] Alan Dundes, The number three in American culture, manuscript, Berkeley, 1968

[4] Robert Eisberg; Fundamentals of modern physics, Wiley and Sons, New York, 1961

[5] Gavin Flood; An introduction to Hinduism, Cambridge University Press, 1996

[6] George Gamow; One, two, three, ...Infinity, The Viking Press, New York, 1947

[7] Stephen Hawking; God created the integers: The mathematical breakthroughs that changed history, Running Press, Philadelphia, 2007

[8] Tom Holland; Rubicon: The last years of the Roman Republic, Random House, 2005

[9] Cornelius Lanczos; Space through the ages, University of NC Press, Rayleigh, 1970

[10] Mario Livio; The equation that could not be solved, Simon & Schuster, New York, 2005

[11] Eli Maori; To infinity and beyond. A cultural history of the infinite, Princeton University Press, New Jersey, 1987

[12] John McLeish; Number. From ancient civilizations to the computer, HarperCollins Publishers, London, 1991

[13] Paul J. Nahin; The story of $\sqrt{-1}$, An imaginary tale, Princeton University Press, Princeton, 1998

[14] Clifford A. Pickover; Keys to infinity, Wiley, New York, 1995

[15] Constance Reid; From zero To infinity, Mathematical Association of America, 1992

[16] Mark Ronan; Symmetry and the Monster, Oxford University Press, 2007

[17] Charles Seife; Zero. The biography of a dangerous idea, Penguin Books, New York, 2000

[18] Simon Singh; Fermat's enigma. The epic quest to solve the world's greatest mathematical problem,

Walker, New York, 1997

[19] Ian Stewart; From here to infinity. A guide to today's mathematics, Oxford University Press, Oxford, 1987

[20] David Foster Wallace; Everything and more. A compact history of ∞, Norton books, New York, 2003

[21] Roger Woodward; The Cambridge companion to Greek Mythology, Cambridge University Press, 2007

Index

ABOUT THE BOOK

This book is for people interested in history, intrigued by philosophy and not adverse to a bit of mathematics. The content is a spectacular journey that starts from the historical and archaeological occurrences of the number three.

The bulk of the book is focused on the bewildering array of mathematical roles the number three plays from elementary arithmetics and geometry to trigonometry and algebra. The discussion is lighthearted and narrative, a highly enjoyable reading.

The journey culminates in the description of the spectacular roles of the number three in our physical lives, from biology through our mechanical world to the planetary motions. In conclusion many of the everyday occurrences of the number three are also discussed.

ABOUT THE AUTHOR

Dr. Louis Komzsik is an accomplished author of several internationally acknowledged mathematical and engineering books, some of them translated to foreign languages.

This book is the outcome of his lifelong fascination with numbers and specifically with the number three. He inclines toward the belief that there is a deep reason for the myriad occurrences of the number three in our lives that we cannot yet fully comprehend.